HEZBOLLAH'S GROWING THREAT AGAINST U.S. NATIONAL SECURITY INTERESTS IN THE MIDDLE EAST

HEARING

BEFORE THE

SUBCOMMITTEE ON THE MIDDLE EAST AND NORTH AFRICA

OF THE

COMMITTEE ON FOREIGN AFFAIRS HOUSE OF REPRESENTATIVES

ONE HUNDRED FOURTEENTH CONGRESS

SECOND SESSION

MARCH 22, 2016

Serial No. 114–163

Printed for the use of the Committee on Foreign Affairs

Available via the World Wide Web: http://www.foreignaffairs.house.gov/ or http://www.gpo.gov/fdsys/

U.S. GOVERNMENT PUBLISHING OFFICE

99–555PDF   WASHINGTON : 2016

For sale by the Superintendent of Documents, U.S. Government Publishing Office
Internet: bookstore.gpo.gov   Phone: toll free (866) 512–1800; DC area (202) 512–1800
Fax: (202) 512–2104   Mail: Stop IDCC, Washington, DC 20402–0001

COMMITTEE ON FOREIGN AFFAIRS

EDWARD R. ROYCE, California, *Chairman*

CHRISTOPHER H. SMITH, New Jersey
ILEANA ROS-LEHTINEN, Florida
DANA ROHRABACHER, California
STEVE CHABOT, Ohio
JOE WILSON, South Carolina
MICHAEL T. McCAUL, Texas
TED POE, Texas
MATT SALMON, Arizona
DARRELL E. ISSA, California
TOM MARINO, Pennsylvania
JEFF DUNCAN, South Carolina
MO BROOKS, Alabama
PAUL COOK, California
RANDY K. WEBER SR., Texas
SCOTT PERRY, Pennsylvania
RON DeSANTIS, Florida
MARK MEADOWS, North Carolina
TED S. YOHO, Florida
CURT CLAWSON, Florida
SCOTT DesJARLAIS, Tennessee
REID J. RIBBLE, Wisconsin
DAVID A. TROTT, Michigan
LEE M. ZELDIN, New York
DANIEL DONOVAN, New York

ELIOT L. ENGEL, New York
BRAD SHERMAN, California
GREGORY W. MEEKS, New York
ALBIO SIRES, New Jersey
GERALD E. CONNOLLY, Virginia
THEODORE E. DEUTCH, Florida
BRIAN HIGGINS, New York
KAREN BASS, California
WILLIAM KEATING, Massachusetts
DAVID CICILLINE, Rhode Island
ALAN GRAYSON, Florida
AMI BERA, California
ALAN S. LOWENTHAL, California
GRACE MENG, New York
LOIS FRANKEL, Florida
TULSI GABBARD, Hawaii
JOAQUIN CASTRO, Texas
ROBIN L. KELLY, Illinois
BRENDAN F. BOYLE, Pennsylvania

AMY PORTER, *Chief of Staff*   THOMAS SHEEHY, *Staff Director*
JASON STEINBAUM, *Democratic Staff Director*

————

SUBCOMMITTEE ON THE MIDDLE EAST AND NORTH AFRICA

ILEANA ROS-LEHTINEN, Florida, *Chairman*

STEVE CHABOT, Ohio
JOE WILSON, South Carolina
DARRELL E. ISSA, California
RANDY K. WEBER SR., Texas
RON DeSANTIS, Florida
MARK MEADOWS, North Carolina
TED S. YOHO, Florida
CURT CLAWSON, Florida
DAVID A. TROTT, Michigan
LEE M. ZELDIN, New York

THEODORE E. DEUTCH, Florida
GERALD E. CONNOLLY, Virginia
BRIAN HIGGINS, New York
DAVID CICILLINE, Rhode Island
ALAN GRAYSON, Florida
GRACE MENG, New York
LOIS FRANKEL, Florida
BRENDAN F. BOYLE, Pennsylvania

CONTENTS

HEZBOLLAH'S GROWING THREAT AGAINST U.S. NATIONAL SECURITY INTERESTS IN THE MIDDLE EAST

TUESDAY, MARCH 22, 2016

House of Representatives,
Subcommittee on the Middle East and North Africa,
Committee on Foreign Affairs,
Washington, DC.

The committee met, pursuant to notice, at 2:30 p.m., in room 2172 Rayburn House Office Building, Hon. Ileana Ros-Lehtinen (chairman of the subcommittee) presiding.

Ms. Ros-Lehtinen. The subcommittee will come to order.

After recognizing myself and Ranking Member Deutch for 5 minutes each for our opening statements, I will then recognize other members seeking recognition for 1 minute.

We will then hear from our witnesses and without objection, witnesses, your prepared statements will be made a part of the record and members may have 5 days in which to insert statements and questions for the record subject to the length limitations in the rules.

Before we begin today, I would just like to say, and I'm sure that I'm speaking on behalf of all of the members, that we condemn in the strongest terms the terrorist attacks in Brussels today and our condolences are with those impacted by this evil and with all of the people of Brussels.

We stand ready, willing and able to assist our European allies with whatever they need to root out these terrorists and hold those responsible accountable.

I think today's attacks and the subject matter of today's hearing only serve to further underscore the need for all of us—the U.S., our allies, all—to do more to combat and destroy ISIS and other terrorist groups like Hezbollah and it has to start with finding a comprehensive plan for Syria that includes defeating all the terror groups and seeing Assad removed from power.

We certainly have trying times ahead but I'm confident that these terrorists will not change our way of life and that freedom and democracy will ultimately triumph over this radical extremism and hatred.

The chair now recognizes herself for 5 minutes. Iran, Syria, Lebanon, Israel—the proxy war between Saudi Arabia and the Arab states and Iran—these are all some of the top priorities for U.S. national security interests in the Middle East.

And one of the common denominators here, one thing at the center of all of this, is the U.S.-designated Foreign Terrorist Organization—FTO—Hezbollah.

This Shi'ite Islamist group is an Iran proxy group that is known to be one of the world's most dangerous and capable terror organizations trained and equipped and funded by Iran's Quds Force.

Hezbollah has been responsible for some of the world's most infamous terror attacks including the 1983 U.S. Marine barracks bombing in Beirut, the 1994 AMIA Jewish community center in Buenos Aires and the bombing of a bus in Bulgaria which targeted Israeli citizens.

But this is just a small fraction of the terror activities as Hezbollah is present around the world including an alarming presence right here in our own hemisphere where it is involved in drug trafficking, smuggling networks and terror operations.

This U.S.-designated FTO has been responsible for provoking war with Israel most recently in the 34-day conflict in 2006 which saw the militant group launch over 4,000 rockets indiscriminately into northern Israel.

Hezbollah is responsible for destabilizing Lebanon's political scene and is growing its influence and presence there, much to the detriment of Lebanon and her people.

Hezbollah was found to be responsible for the assassination of the former prime minister in 2005 and, of course, Hezbollah has been used by the Iranian regime as ground forces to protect the regime's interest in Syria.

With all of this it is clear that Hezbollah represents a growing threat to our national security interests, especially in the wake of the sanctions relief that the Iranian Government has received as part of this weak and dangerous nuclear agreement.

Hezbollah receives financial and materiel support from Iran and now with the regime receiving this financial windfall of over $100 billion, it is not only reasonable to expect that Iran will increase its support for its proxy, it is as near of a guarantee as one can have.

With the terror group being such a vital arm of Iran's foreign policy agenda we would be silly and ignorant to expect that it wouldn't use this as an opportunity to strengthen this vital extension of its damaging apparatus.

This is likely one of the major driving forces behind the Gulf countries and the Arab League making the decision to designate Hezbollah as a terrorist organization.

This designation, regardless of the motivations, was a step in the right direction and we'd like to see more of that from our GCC partners in fighting terror groups like Hezbollah and that includes doing more to combat terror financing in those countries.

But it is encouraging and we should seek to work with them in an effort to cut off Hezbollah's support from Iran and eliminate the threat that it poses.

Saudi Arabia has cut its military assistance to Lebanon in part because of Hezbollah's undue influence in Beirut and the Lebanese Government. That undue influence led the Lebanese justice minister to resign.

This should be sounding alarm bells for the administration. Not only is it allowing Iran and Hezbollah to push us around in Syria but it is allowing Iran to grow its influence in Lebanon and extend its grasp in the region.

Now we have Hezbollah on the border with Israel in Lebanon and we have Hezbollah in the Golan Heights, and just because it is preoccupied with the fight in Syria doesn't mean it has turned a blind eye on Israel.

Make no mistake about it. The cease fire between Israel and Hezbollah has nothing to do with Hezbollah not wanting to fight Israel. It has everything to do with the terror group restocking and building up its missile and rocket stockpile so that it can once again launch an all-out attack against the Jewish state.

In fact, with all the chaos going on in Syria right now, it has helped Iran and the Assad regime in their efforts to smuggle more weapons and more ammunition and more sophisticated weapons systems to the terror group and that includes some advanced Russian-made weapons systems, which could seriously jeopardize Israel's security.

Anytime we have Russia, Iran and Hezbollah operating in the same theater with the same objectives, it cannot be good for the security and the stability of the region.

It is an imminent threat to our friend and ally, the democratic Jewish state of Israel, and it is a great threat to our national security interests in the region as the proxy war between Iran and some of our GCC allies threatens to escalate.

The Obama administration needs to do more to counter Hezbollah and Iran in Syria, which means delivering a comprehensive strategy to defeat ISIS and the Assad-Hezbollah-Iran nexus.

It needs to do more to take action to combat the weapons transfers from Russia to Iran and to Hezbollah in Syria. The President needs to use the tools at his disposal to sanction Hezbollah and cut off its network, and the President needs to realize that foregoing old alliances in the region to legitimize relations with and legitimize itself, the Iranian regime, is a strategic calamity that will have terrible consequences for the region and for our national security interests for years to come.

With that, I'm pleased to recognize the ranking member, my friend, Mr. Deutch of Florida.

Mr. DEUTCH. Thank you very much, Madame Chairman.

I'd also like to just take a moment to say that we stand with the people of Brussels, the people of Belgium and all those who are resolute in battling ISIS and the terrorist groups that cowardly launch attacks on innocent civilians.

It will not win, not in Belgium, not in Turkey, not in Cote d'Ivoire, not in Israel, nowhere, and our thoughts and prayers go out to the victims—today's victims and to their families.

Thank you to our witnesses. It's a pleasure to welcome you all back to our subcommittee and I thank the chairman for convening today's hearing to examining the terrorist organization Hezbollah whose dangerous behavior poses a threat in nearly every corner of the globe.

Hezbollah was founded as a resistance group against Israel, a group dedicated to the destruction of the state of Israel.

Today, its activities are broad and they are wide. Hezbollah has become Iran's proxy terrorist using Iranian dollars to launch attacks around the world just as they use Iranian weapons to kill Syrians.

Hezbollah is responsible for the 1992 Israeli Embassy bombing in Argentina which killed 29 people, the 1994 bombing of the AMIA Jewish center that killed 85 people. It attacked a bus of tourists in Bulgaria in 2012.

Since 2008, attacks plotted by Hezbollah have been foiled in Cyprus, in Azerbaijan, in Georgia and in Turkey. And in 2012 a Hezbollah plot to assassinate the Ambassador of Saudi Arabia right here in Washington was uncovered.

This attack, had it gone forward, would have resulted in the deaths of innocent civilians here in our nation's capital. And while Hezbollah has been a designated U.S. Foreign Terrorist Organization since 1997, it still operates freely around the world as a so-called political group—a political group.

The distinction between Hezbollah's political and military wings allows the group to fundraise throughout Europe and Latin America.

The Hezbollah International Financing Prevention Act, which I was proud to introduce with Chairman Royce, Ranking Member Engel and my friend, Mr. Meadows, has been signed into law and would help crack down on Hezbollah's use of the banking system as well as its other funding sources from narco-trafficking to money laundering.

Now, today's hearing comes on the heels of two surprising announcements—the designation of Hezbollah as a terrorist organization by the Gulf Cooperation Council followed by the same designation by the Arab League.

These actions are a clear indication of just how dangerous Hezbollah has become as it does Iran's dirty work throughout the Middle East.

Iran has a long history of meddling in neighboring countries with hopes of destabilizing governments and inciting unrest among Shi'ite populations.

After the conclusion of the nuclear agreement, there is increasing concern about the kind of damage an Iran with access to billions of dollars in sanctions relief could do.

But Hezbollah is not just a threat to Israel and to Arab states. This murderous group has a history of attacking American citizens and American interests.

Since its inception in 1982, Hezbollah has attacked American citizens in the bombing of the U.S. Embassy in Beirut in 1983, killing 63 including 17 Americans, the U.S. Marine barracks bombing in October 1983 which killed 241 American and 58 French servicemen, the bombing of the U.S. Embassy annex in Beirut in 1984 which killed 24, the hijacking of TWA 847 in 1985 in which a Navy diver was shot in the head and his body dumped on the Tarmac, and the Khobar Towers attack in Saudi Arabia in 1996 that killed 19 U.S. airmen.

Desperate to hang on to its best friend, Bashar al-Assad, Iran dispatched Hezbollah mercenaries to Syria nearly 5 years ago. Hezbollah has sustained the regime's grip on power and aided in the slaughter of hundreds of thousands of innocent Syrians by providing Assad with somewhere between 6,000 and 8,000 fighters.

Just this week, Hezbollah leader Hassan Nasrallah vowed that his fighters would press on in Syria even as Assad loses his support from the Russian air force.

The conflict in Syria has delivered an influx of new weapons into the region, increasing the chances that dangerous chemical or advanced precision weapons had fallen into Hezbollah's hands.

Already Hezbollah is reportedly in possession of Russian-designed surface-to-air shoulder-mounted missile systems and with an arsenal of well over 100,000 missiles, which are, according to Nasrallah, capable of reaching every corner of Israel, it is troubling to imagine these rockets with precision capabilities or Hezbollah with a stockpile of chemical weapons that could one day be used against Israel.

The U.S. must lead the efforts to interdict Iranian weapons as they make their way to Hezbollah for use in Syria and against Israel. We have tremendous cooperation with Israel in these efforts but the international community under the mandate of U.N. Security Council Resolution 1701, which calls for the de-arming of Hezbollah, must step up these efforts.

The Security Council must do more to ensure that Security Council resolutions are implemented. The U.N. peacekeeping mission in Lebanon does not have the ability to de-arm Hezbollah. There is no enforcement mechanism.

Hezbollah has a stranglehold on Lebanon, the country is paralyzed because Hezbollah essentially functions as a state within a state. The political stalemate has persisted for nearly 2 years with the government unable to select a President.

Moreover, the Lebanese Armed Forces must be the sole security apparatus in the country. I was pleased to see the Security Council reaffirm this last week reiterating their strong support for the territorial integrity, sovereignty and political independence of Lebanon and underscoring the crucial role played by the Lebanese Armed Forces and security forces in extending and sustaining the authority of the state in supporting the country's stability.

As long as Hezbollah remains in Syria, a threat to Lebanon remains. Retaliatory bombings have struck Beirut, the country is buckling under the weight of over 1 million refugees and Hezbollah is desperate to see its lifeline to Iran preserved.

This makes a political solution that removes Bashar al-Assad from power all the more important for regional international security. Without Assad, the Hezbollah-Iran nexus is inherently weakened.

Madam Chairman, it is time for the world to call Hezbollah what it is—a terrorist organization that murders innocent civilians at the behest of Iran.

I hope today will give us new insight into how we can beat Iranian support for Hezbollah and curb the menacing group's activities in the Middle East and around the world, and I yield back.

Thank you.

Ms. ROS-LEHTINEN. Thank you very much, Mr. Deutch.

And seeing no member request for time, we are so pleased to get to our witnesses and I thank the witnesses and the audience for their patience, as we had a series of votes.

We are pleased to welcome back Dr. Matthew Levitt, Director of the Stein Program on Counterterrorism and Intelligence for the Washington Institute for Near East Policy.

Previously, Dr. Levitt has served as the Deputy Assistant Secretary of Intelligence and Analysis at the U.S. Department of the Treasury, a branch chief under the Director of National Intelligence and a Counterterrorism Advisor to the State Department's Special Envoy to the Middle East. Welcome, Dr. Levitt.

We would also like to welcome back Dr. Tony Badran, a research fellow at the Foundation for Defense of Democracies. Dr. Badran focuses on Lebanon, Syria and Hezbollah.

As an expert on U.S. foreign policy toward Syria and nonstate actors and terrorist groups, Dr. Badran has—well, I made you a doctor, that's not bad—has written extensively—my arm hurts, maybe you could take a look at it—extensively in Hezbollah.

And lastly but not least, we would like to welcome back Dr. Daniel Byman, who is a professor in the Security Studies Program at Georgetown University School of Foreign Service and the research director for the Saban Center for the Middle East Policy at the Brookings Institution.

Dr. Byman previously served as a professional staff member for the National Commission on Terrorist Attacks on the United States and the joint 9/11 inquiry staff of the House and Senate Intelligence Committees.

Thank you, gentlemen. Your prepared remarks will be made a part of the record and please feel free to summarize. Dr. Levitt, we will begin with you.

STATEMENT OF MATTHEW LEVITT, PH.D., DIRECTOR AND FROMER-WEXLER FELLOW, STEIN PROGRAM ON COUNTER-TERRORISM AND INTELLIGENCE, WASHINGTON INSTITUTE FOR NEAR EAST POLICY

Mr. LEVITT. Thank you very much, Chairman Ros-Lehtinen and Ranking Member Deutch, members of the committee.

It's a pleasure to be here. I, too, would like to just make a comment about Brussels. I was in Brussels last week meeting with counterterrorism officials including with officials as they were planning the first raid last Tuesday.

But I also had the opportunity while there to talk to them about Hezbollah and there is some silver lining here, because due to Hezbollah's tremendous investment in international organized crime, going up to the highest levels of Hezbollah, we now have an opportunity to work with Europeans, even within the context of a European Union designation of Hezbollah that is partial, just the military and terrorist wings, as if such a distinction exists.

Hezbollah will be the first to tell you it does not, and so maybe this is something we should push on again.

But even where things are, we are seeing tremendous cooperation with them on these cases. The fact is that Hezbollah has branched out and experienced a regional transformation.

We see the designation by the GCC and Arab League and it's because of an increased amount of Hezbollah activity in the region, not just the long history of Hezbollah in the Gulf, and to be clear, for example, just 2 months after the finalization day of JCPOA we had the arrest of Mughassil who was one of the masterminds of the Khobar Towers bombing that you both mentioned.

Hezbollah's transformation has, clearly, taken it to Syria. It has taken it to Iraq in small numbers. But, for example, the Treasury Department designated al-Inmaa Group, a Beirut-based engineering company which has been opening up basically fronts to finance and support Hezbollah activities, a small footprint in Yemen, which is most noticeable for the very high ranking Hezbollah operatives that they have sent there.

When Hezbollah sends a special operations commander like Abu Ali Tabatabai to Yemen, that means that Yemen means something to them, even if they're not sending large numbers of people.

Hezbollah's global criminal networks are on the increase and it's important to note that they rely sometimes on what we call these criminal super facilitators who can move and launder tremendous amounts of money in and out of Europe, in and out of the United States.

It's important to note that the Department of Justice, the U.S. Drug Enforcement Administration, has been targeting a whole host of these actors.

To be clear, we don't actually know what this unit within Hezbollah calls itself. But U.S. law enforcement, for lack of a better term, came up with a name called the Business Affairs Component—the BAC—which to be clear is not operating on behalf of Hezbollah's political wing, for its social welfare wing, but it is specifically under and providing facilitation and finance for the terrorist wing, the Islamic Jihad organization, the external security organization, and was founded, according to the GOA, by Imad Mughniyah himself before he was killed in 2008. That's how far back this organization goes.

In terms of the Western Hemisphere, the BAC has established working relationships according to DOJ with South American drug cartels that supply cocaine to drug markets in both the U.S. and Europe.

The BAC then launders these drugs through well-known black market peso exchange and other vehicles. This has come close to the United States as well. One of the most important arrests we've made was of an individual who we lured to Atlanta, Imam Kubaisi, in October 2015, just 3 weeks after the end of the 60-day congressional review period for JCPOA. She was arrested in Atlanta.

She was arraigned on money laundering conspiracy charges, unlicensed firearms dealing, conspiracy for laundering funds she believed to be drug money and for arranging for the sale of thousands of firearms including military assault rifles, machine guns and sniper rifles to criminal groups in Iran and Lebanon, including Hezbollah. She also was trying to procure airplane parts for Iran.

And meanwhile, as associate of hers, Joseph Asmar, was arrested in Paris—again, underscoring the tremendous law enforcement cooperation we're seeing with key European allies.

According to the Department of Justice, Kubaisi and Asmar explained that they could arrange for places from South America—planes, that is, from South America laden with multi-ton shipments of cocaine to land safely in Africa as a transit point before the drugs were smuggled to the United States and to Europe.

DEA recording of the conversation of these two individuals with a DEA undercover discussing their money laundering network and the services they provided to drug traffickers, terrorist organizations and other criminal groups including places—in places like Lebanon, Iran, France, Belgium, again, Bulgaria, Benin, the DRC, Ghana, Nigeria, Cyprus and, yes, across the United States.

We see Hezbollah not only engaging in facilitation but also operational activity, the latest plot to be thwarted in Cyprus with Hussein Bassam Abdallah, a dual Lebanese-Canadian citizen involved in the stockpiling of over eight tons of ammonia nitrate, and according to intelligence officials that was intended not just for Cyprus but for further operations in Europe.

The fact is that there are activities here in the Western Hemisphere we need to be extremely cognizant of. The most recent plot to be thwarted was in Peru. The individual who was arrested, Mohamad Amadar, had married a dual Peruvian-American citizen who was a resident in Miami.

But perhaps the most—the thing we need to be most concerned about and which perhaps you haven't heard is that the person who was the handler for Mohamad Amadar, who met with him personally in Turkey, was Salman Al-Redda.

Salman Al-Redda has been indicted for his role in the 1994 bombing of the AMIA attacks. He came and went throughout South America in the years followed, never arrested, and he has become one of the absolute top—perhaps the top three or four Islamic jihad organization Hezbollah terrorist wing operatives personally in charge of operations in South America, and those operations continue.

My time is over, but I'd like—if you're interested I'm happy to tell you about some of the other things that Treasury, the State Department and the Department of Justice are doing.

There's good things happening from the United States regarding Hezbollah. But my time is over. I want to thank you for having me once more.

[The prepared statement of Mr. Levitt follows:]

Hezbollah's Growing Threat against U.S. National Security Interests in the Middle East

Dr. Matthew Levitt

Fromer-Wexler Fellow and Director, Stein Program on Counterterrorism and Intelligence,
The Washington Institute for Near East Policy; Author of *Hezbollah: The Global Footprint of Lebanon's Party of God* (Georgetown University Press).

Testimony submitted to the House Foreign Affairs Subcommittee on the Middle East and North Africa

March 22, 2016

Chairman Ileana Ros-Lehtinen, Ranking Member Deutch, and Members of the Committee, thank you for this opportunity to appear before you today to discuss the relationship between Hezbollah and Iran, which is only growing strong in the wake of the nuclear deal with Iran.

Barely ten days after the JCPOA was signed in Vienna, Hezbollah General Secretary Hassan Nasrallah stated that, "Iran's relationship with its allies is based on ideological grounds and come before the political interests." [1] In April 2015, Nasrallah noted that even under sanctions Iran funded its allies, and anticipated that a now "rich and powerful Iran, which will be open to the world" would be able to do even more: "I say that in the next phase Iran will be able to stand by its allies, friends, the people in the region, and especially the resistance in Palestine and the Palestinian people more than any time in the past, and this is what the others are afraid of." [2]

Hezbollah officials are comfortable and confident that Iran will not abandon the group. As one Hezbollah official told *al Monitor*: "'Hezbollah is more than just an ally for Iran.' The relationship is similar to 'that between father and son'... Hezbollah's importance as an ally for Iran in the region has also become quite clear ... The group has played a pivotal role in preserving the leadership of President Bashar al-Assad in Syria, Iran's No. 1 regional ally. Hezbollah has sent military personnel to Iraq to join the fight against Islamic State terrorists, helping to prevent an extremist takeover that would pose a dangerous national security threat for neighboring Iran." [3]

Hezbollah and Iran's cooperation in Syria offers a tangible indication of their increasingly intimate operational collaboration since the nuclear deal. Unofficially, Hezbollah has been on the ground fighting to prop up the Assad regime since 2011 at Tehran's behest. It has been a costly venture for Hezbollah, losing as many as a third of its fighting forces according to a December 2015 estimate. [4] Soon, Hezbollah forces were joined in Syria by Iranian troops and advisors on the ground. By October 2015, media reported that "Hundreds of Iranian troops have arrived in Syria in the last 10 days and will soon join government forces and their Lebanese Hezbollah allies in a major ground offensive." [5]

And while it is by far the most significant, Syria is not the only regional conflict where Iran and Hezbollah are working together. In Yemen there have been claims that Hezbollah is on the ground fighting and training the Houthi rebels with Iran's blessing. It has long been suspected that Iran and Hezbollah played a role in supporting the Houthis, either financially or technically, as one Hezbollah commander described it, "Houthis and Hizbollah trained together for the past 10 years. "They trained with us in Iran, then we trained them here and in Yemen."[6]

Further indication of Iran and Hezbollah's continued working relationship can be seen in Iran's stern response to the GCC's designation of Hezbollah. Major General Hassan Firouzabadi, chief of staff of the Iranian Armed Forces responded by declaring, "Despite efforts by the House of Saud [Saudi Arabia] and its regional and trans-regional allies, Hezbollah's deep-seated position will remain intact."[7] Meanwhile, Iran Foreign Ministry spokesman Jaberi Ansari accused Arab states of aligning themselves with the "occupiers of Palestine… Those who are behind the move are knowingly or unknowingly undermining the interests of the Muslim nations."[8]

Behind the GCC's Terrorist Designation of Hezbollah

The GCC decision to blacklist Hezbollah goes back at least three years. In June 2013, the Gulf Cooperation Council (GCC) countries came to the unanimous conclusion that Lebanese Hezbollah is a terrorist organization, and several member states began taking discrete actions against the groups' supporters in their countries.[9] For example, in May 2014, Saudi Arabia withdrew the business license of a Lebanese national, who reportedly had ties to Hezbollah.[10] But at the time, the GCC was trying to woo Iran away from its then-deepening commitment to the Assad regime in Syria, which Tehran largely accomplished by dispatching its Lebanese proxy, Hezbollah, to defend the Assad regime. GCC Secretary-General Abdullatif Al-Zayani said at the time that the GCC was ready to engage Iran in dialogue if Tehran were to changes its policies. That did not happen.

Fast forward to March 2016, and the GCC has now formalized its designation of Hezbollah as a terrorist organization for committing hostile acts within GCC member states' borders. As GCC Secretary General Abdullatif al-Zayani said in a public statement, "As the militia continues its terrorist practices, the GCC states have decided to label it a terrorist organization and will take the necessary measures to implement its decision in this regard based on anti-terrorism laws applied in the GCC and similar international laws."[11] GCC states are still concerned about Hezbollah activities in Syria, and the move is also part of the broader sectarian and geopolitical tensions between Saudi Arabia and Iran (the designation followed Saudi Arabia's decision to cut off some $3 billion dollars in military aid to Lebanon in February), but there is also reason for GCC states to be increasingly concerned about Hezbollah activities in the Gulf.[12]

Hezbollah has long been active beyond Lebanon's borders, including in the Gulf. According to the CIA, Hezbollah branches have operated in the Gulf since the late 1980s.[13] In

1986, Manama began to crack down on Bahraini Hezbollah; a year later, it arrested and tried fifty-nine accused members.[14] Yet the group was far from beaten -- in March 1997, Kuwaiti intelligence arrested thirteen Bahrainis and two Iraqis in Kuwait City, at the time operating under the name "Hezbollah Gulf."[15] Correspondence seized at their homes revealed that they had connections with individuals in Damascus, Syria, and Qom, Iran, and that they were raising money to send back to Bahrain. Other evidence suggested the group was getting their directives straight from Iran's Ministry of Intelligence and Security.

Saudi Hezbollah carried out its first attack on a petroleum facility inside the kingdom in May 1987.[16] Ten months later, Saudi Hezbollah claimed responsibility for an explosion at the Sadaf petrochemical plant in Jubail. Saudi authorities responded forcefully, arresting and executing a number of suspected militants. In retaliation Saudi Hezbollah declared war on "the House of Saud," and assassinated Abdulgani Bedawi, the second secretary at the Saudi embassy in Turkey. Two months later, they attempted to assassinate Ahmed al-Amri, the second secretary at the Saudi mission in Karachi, Pakistan, who survived but with serious injuries. Then, on January 4, 1989, Saleh Abdullah al-Maliki, the third secretary at the Saudi embassy in Bangkok, was shot and killed outside his home. The most well-known Hezbollah attack on Saudi interests was the June 1996 Khobar Towers bombing, which killed 19 U.S. servicemen and an unspecified number of Saudi civilians in a nearby park and wounded another 372 Americans.[17]

In December 12, 1983, Hezbollah and Iraqi Da'wa operatives together carried out a series of seven coordinated bombings in Kuwait, killing six people and wounding nearly ninety more. The targets included the American and French embassies, the Kuwait airport, the grounds of the Raytheon Corporation, a Kuwait National Petroleum Company oil rig, and a government-owned power station. Ultimately, seventeen convicted terrorists were jailed in Kuwait -- the Kuwait 17, as they came to be called -- including several Hezbollah members.[18] Over the following years, Hezbollah would carry out many more attacks, at home and abroad, seeking the release of their jailed comrades, who included Mustapha Badreddine—brother-in-law of Hezbollah terrorist chief Imad Mughniyeh. Following Mughniyeh's 2008 assassination, Badreddine assumed leadership of Hezbollah's terrorist wing and later of its militia battalion is Syria as well.

More recently, Hezbollah established a dedicated unit—Unit 3800—to support Iraqi Shia militias targeting coalition forces during the Iraq war, which mostly focused on training Shia militias but also engaged in operations targeting American and British forces in Iraq.[19]

Then came the war in Syria, which has dramatically changed Hezbollah (see below). Once focused on jockeying for political power in Lebanon and fighting Israel, the group is now a regional player engaged in conflicts far beyond Lebanon's borders, often in cooperation with Iran.

The GCC's decision to blacklist Hezbollah has been coming from some time, as underscored by the GCC's more informal June 2013 determination that Hezbollah is a terrorist group. In 2014, Dubai's police chief Lieutenant General Dahi Khalfan accused Hezbollah of training local Shia militants who killed three Bahraini policemen in a bombing attack.[20]

Since then, Hezbollah has activities in the region have increased. Over the past few months, Hezbollah operatives have been arrested in a series of operations, including in Kuwait,[21] Bahrain,[22] and the United Arab Emirates.[23]

In June 2015, the Kuwaiti Ministry of Interior blacklisted nearly a dozen Lebanese journalists for suspected links to Hezbollah. Five of the Lebanese journalists will not have their residencies renewed and two others were given one month to leave the country. Authorities stated that evidence demonstrated the blacklisted individuals provided financial, media and political support to Hezbollah.[24]Additionally, the Kuwaiti General Directorate of State Security has prepared a list to ban people with links to Hezbollah from entering Kuwait, as well as to deport those already in the country.[25] In June 2015, the U.S. Treasury designated Hezbollah operatives who were using their business interests in Iraq to raise funds and provide logistical support to the group's activities there.[26] On February 26, 2016 Saudi Arabia designated four companies and three Lebanese businessmen over their ties to Hezbollah.[27] Although the United States had already designated these same entities a year prior, it was still an indication of the rising attention the Saudi-led GCC was paying to Hezbollah.[28]

All of these actions provide context to the geo-political and sectarian tensions currently rising between Saudi Arabia and its Gulf Allies and Iran. These tensions can be seen playing out across the region but peaked with the execution of Sheik Nimr al-Nimr and the subsequent storming of two Saudi Arabian diplomatic communities in Iran.[29] Days later, the Saudis sought Arab League and Organization of Islamic Cooperation condemnations of both the embassy attacks and of Iranian and Hezbollah activities in the region. When Lebanon offered only "solidarity," but not "condemnation," the Saudis responded by cutting off monetary support to Lebanon and pulling funds from Lebanese banks.[30] Bahrain joined Saudi Arabia in its retaliation by issuing travel advisory warnings citizens against traveling to Lebanon, while UAE said it would ban Emiratis from visiting the country, further exacerbating the sectarian and geopolitical tensions in the region.[31]

While Hezbollah leader Hassan Nasrallah attempted to deflect the GCC blacklisting as an example of Israeli machinations, the truth is although the timing of recent GCC actions against Hezbollah is largely a factor of regional sectarian tensions, Hezbollah and Iran have been increasingly engaged in activities in Gulf countries over the past few years and months.[32] Coming against the backdrop of the Iran nuclear deal, which has raised concerns among Gulf States that Iran will use an influx of funds to destabilize GCC countries, Gulf States are especially sensitive to the activities of Iran and its proxies in the region.[33]

The bottom line is while the GCC terrorism designation of Hezbollah is indeed a function of the recent sectarian and geopolitical tensions between the Sunni Gulf States and Shia Iran; it is also more than that. It is the cumulative result of a long history of Hezbollah activity the region, and it comes on the heels of the nuclear deal with Iran and the recent spike in Iranian and Hezbollah-linked plots across the Gulf.

Hezbollah's Transformation

Hezbollah's recently increased activities in the Gulf are just one manifestation of the uptick in the group's global activities over the past few years, which has continued in the period since the signing of the JCPOA. Hezbollah is now a regional power player entrenched in military conflicts in multiple countries plus more covert terror plots and criminal enterprises throughout the world.

Syria

The war in Syria has dramatically changed Hezbollah. Once limited to jockeying for political power in Lebanon and fighting Israel, the group is now a regional player engaged in conflicts far beyond its historical area of operations (read Iraq and Yemen), often in cooperation with Iran. The strongest indicators of Hezbollah's transformation are structural. Since 2013, the group has added two new commands—the first on the Lebanese–Syrian border, the second within Syria itself—to its existing bases in southern and eastern Lebanon.

In establishing its new presence in Syria, Hezbollah has transferred key personnel from its traditionally paramount Southern Command, along Lebanon's border with Israel. Mustafa Badreddine, the head of Hezbollah's foreign terrorist operations, began coordinating Hezbollah military activities in Syria in 2012 and now heads the group's Syrian command. Badreddine is a Hezbollah veteran implicated in the 1983 bombing of U.S. barracks in Beirut, the 2005 assassination of former Lebanese Prime Minister Rafik Hariri, and terrorist bombings in , among other attacks. His appointment is the strongest sign Hezbollah can give of its commitment to Syria's civil war.

In addition to the traditional Lebanese Hezbollah, who has been deploying fighters to Syria since 2011, Islamic Revolutionary Guard Corps (IRGC) General Hossein Hamedani declared in May 2014 that Iran had formed "a second Hezbollah in Syria." In early 2014, several Shiite militias in Syria began to call themselves, "Hezbollah fi Suriya," or Hezbollah in Syria. Inspired by the success of Lebanese Hezbollah, Iran had begun to build a Syrian wing of the movement, to "carry out ideological as well as other regional power-projection goals."[34] While most of their actions so far have been limited to Syria, Hezbollah fi Suriya has made calls to unify with others in Iraq as well. The Hezbollahzation of these groups, in name, structure, and allegiance, signifies a major accomplishment for Tehran, allowing Iran to preserve harder-core influence and more effectively project power within Syria.[35]

Iraq

Even as it deepens its activities in Syria, Hezbollah continues to aid Shiite militias in Iraq, sending small numbers of skilled trainers to train Shia militias and help defend Shiite shrines there. Indeed, Hassan Nasrallah admitted on March 6, 2016 that Hezbollah had covertly dispatched Hezbollah operatives to Iraq, "In Iraq, we fought under the Iraqi command and we did not interfere in their affairs. It is an ethical, humanitarian and pan-Arab duty," and he continued to say that some Hezbollah fighters remained in Iraq now because the Islamic State is still there. [36]

According to the U.S. Department of the Treasury, Hezbollah has also invested in commercial front organizations to support its operations in Iraq. Hezbollah member Adham Tabaja, the majority owner of the Lebanon-based real estate and construction firm Al-Inmaa Group for Tourism Works, has exploited the firm's Iraqi subsidiaries to fund Hezbollah, with the assistance of Kassem Hejeij, a Lebanese businessman tied to Hezbollah, and Husayn Ali Faour, a member of Hezbollah's overseas terrorism unit.[37]

Yemen

On February 24, 2016, the Gulf-backed government in Yemen asserted it had physical evidence of "Hezbollah of training the Houthi rebels and fighting alongside them in attacks on Saudi Arabia's border."[38] Although the number of fighters Hezbollah has sent to Yemen to assist the Houthis may be small, that is certainly not a reflection of the importance with which they view the civil war there. Take for instance Khalil Harb, a former special operations commander and a close adviser to Nasrallah, oversees Hezbollah's activities in Yemen—managing the transfer of funds to the organization within the country—and travels frequently to Tehran to coordinate Hezbollah activities with Iranian officials.[39] Given his experience working with other terrorist organizations, his close relations with Iranian and Hezbollah leaders, and his expertise in special operations and training, appointing Harb to work in Yemen no doubt made a great deal of sense to Hezbollah.

Harb, however, is not the most senior operative dispatched to Yemen by Hezbollah. In the spring of 2015, Hezbollah sent Abu Ali Tabtabai, the senior commander formerly stationed in Syria, to upgrade the group's training program for Yemen's Houthi rebels, which reportedly involves schooling them in guerilla tactics. "Sending in Tabtabai [to Yemen] is a sign of a major Hezbollah investment and commitment," an Israeli official told me. "The key question is how long someone of Tabtabai's stature will stay."[40]

Hezbollah's activities in Yemen are done at Iran's behest, and there is no doubt Iran views Yemen as an important battlefield. In September 2015, an Iranian vessel loaded with weapons and destined for the Houthis was intercepted off the coast of Oman by the Saudi-led coalition. According to the coalition forces that seized the vessel, "14 Iranian sailors were detained on the boat, which was carrying 18 anti-armored Concourse shells, 54 anti-tank shells, shell-battery kits, firing guidance systems, launchers and batteries for binoculars."[41]

Global Networks

To carry further its operational objections, Hezbollah relies on a worldwide network of supporters and sympathizers to provide financial, logistical, and operational support. These include both informal networks of supporters and centrally-run enterprises that effectively operate like international organized criminal organizations. The former provide small level financial or other support, as they are able. But the latter are relied upon for multi-million dollar funding schemes, for logistical support activities like setting up front and cover organizations, and to procure weapons, dual-use items, false documents, and more for the group. Of the former, few tend to be formal networks; often they are intentionally structured to be opaquely affiliated with Hezbollah as to avoid detection. But the latter, which also rely on relationships with criminal "super facilitators" who can move and launder massive amounts of money, for example, are involved in large-scale money laundering, drug smuggling, and arms sales.

Consider the recent arrests by the US Drug Enforcement Administration (DEA) and Europol that targeted what U.S. law enforcement now refer to as the Business Affairs Component (BAC) of Hezbollah's terrorist wing, the Islamic Jihad Organization (also known as the External Security Organization). Engaging in drug trafficking and drug smuggling, U.S. officials report that the BAC was founded by deceased Hezbollah Senior Leader Imad Mughniyah and currently operates under the control of senior Hezbollah official Abdallah Safieddine and recently designated Specially Designated Global Terrorist (SDGT) Adham Tabaja.[42]

The BAC established working relationships with South American drug cartels that supplied cocaine to drug markets in both the US and Europe. The BAC would then launder the drug proceeds through the well-known Black Market Peso Exchange. In late January 2016, the DEA and Customs and Border Protection coordinated with multiple foreign counterparts to arrest top leaders of Hezbollah's BAC, including U.S.-designated SDGT Mohamad Noureddine, who has worked directly with Hezbollah's financial apparatus to transfer Hezbollah funds via his Lebanon-based company Trade Point International S.A.R.L. and maintained direct ties to Hezbollah commercial and terrorist elements in both Lebanon and Iraq.[43] United States Department of Treasury similarly targeted Noureddine and his accomplice Hamdi Zaher El Dine and their company, Trade Point International S.A.R.L.[44]

Hezbollah's aggressive and ongoing procurement efforts have not been reigned in since the signing of the JCPOA, but have actually expanded in scope. These aggressive efforts span the globe, but have been especially pronounced in Europe and South America. Outside of the BAC arrests, United States Department of Treasury designated Hezbollah procurement agent Fadi Hussein Serhan, his company Vatech SARL, Hezbollah procurement agent Adel Mohamad Cherri and his company Le-Hua Electronics Field Co. Limited, and two companies owned or controlled by Specially Designated Global Terrorist and Hezbollah procurement agent Ali Zeaiter.[45]

Vatech SARL, run by Fadi Serhan, was designated for purchasing sensitive technology and equipment, including but not limited to UAVs on behalf of Hezbollah. Serhan sought these products from companies in the US, Europe, Asia and the Middle East. Adel Mohamad Cherri was attempting to procure a variety of electronics from China and send them to the Houthis in Yemen by using his company, Le-Hua Electronic Field Co. Ali Zeaiter's two companies, Aero Skyone Co. Limited and Labico SAL Offshore, were designated for again trying to procure UAV-related equipment through Europe and Asia.[46]

Investigation into Hezbollah BAC finance and facilitation networks has touched the United States as well. In October 2015, U.S. officials arrested Iman Kobeissi in Atlanta, Georgia. Kobeissi was arraigned on money laundering conspiracy charges, unlicensed firearms dealing, conspiracy for laundering funds she believed to be drug money, and for arranging for the sale of thousands of firearms, including military assault rifles, machine guns, and sniper rifles, to criminal groups in Iran and Lebanon, including Hezbollah. The same day, her Hezbollah associate, Joseph Asmar, was arrested in Paris and charged with money laundering conspiracy.[47]

Kobeissi informed a DEA undercover agent posing as a narcotics trafficker that her Hezbollah associates sought to purchase cocaine, weapons, and ammunition. Asmar, an attorney, discussed potential narcotics deals with a DEA undercover agent and suggested he could use his connections with Hezbollah to provide security for narcotics shipments. According to the Department of Justice, "Kobeissi and Asmar explained that they could arrange for places from South America laden with multi-ton shipments of cocaine to land safely in Africa as a transit point before the drugs were smuggled to the United States or Europe." In the DEA recording of the conversation the two discussed their money laundering network and the services they provided to drug traffickers, terrorist organizations, and other criminal groups in Lebanon, Iran,

France, Belgium, Bulgaria, Benin, the Democratic Republic of the Congo, Ghana, Nigeria, Cypress, and cities across the United States.[48]

Cyprus 2.0: Looking toward Europe

Europe has not only served as a procurement destination for Hezbollah but also as a place to carry out operations (Bulgaria, Cyprus) and as a launching point for potential attacks elsewhere. While nuclear negotiations were underway in May of 2015, a Hezbollah plot was disrupted in Larnaca, Cyprus. Hussein Bassam Abdallah, a dual Lebanese-Canadian citizen, stockpiled 8.2 tons of ammonium nitrate, a popular chemical explosive.[49] Abdallah pled guilty to all eight charges against him—including participation in a terrorist group (read: Hezbollah), possessing explosives, and conspiracy to commit a crime.[50] It was the second time in three years that a Cypriot court has sentenced a Hezbollah operative to prison for plotting an attack in Cyprus. The arrest of Abdallah was also an indication that regardless of the ongoing nuclear negotiations and the EU's July 2013 announcement to designate Hezbollah's military wing had not stopped or even slowed Hezbollah's momentum throughout Europe. According to Israeli investigators familiar with the arrest, Hezbollah, was using Cyprus as a "point of export" from which to funnel explosives elsewhere for a series of attacks in Europe.[51] In the words of Israeli Defense Minister Moshe Yaalon, Cypriot authorities had "defeated attempts by Hezbollah and Iran to establish a terror infrastructure" on the island that aimed to expand "throughout Europe."[52]

Hezbollah Operations in South America

Last week marked the 24th anniversary of Hezbollah's 1992 bombing of the Israeli embassy in Buenos Aires. Less than two years later, Hezbollah and Iran teamed up again in the 1994 bombing of the Asociación Mutual Israelita Argentina (AMIA).

Meanwhile, Hezbollah activities in the region have picked up pace significantly. In its 2014 annual terrorism report the State Department highlighted the financial support networks Hezbollah maintains in places like Latin America and Africa. The report concluded that Hezbollah remains, "capable of operating around the globe."[53] This conclusion was underscored in November 2014 when Brazilian police reports revealed that Hezbollah helped a Brazilian prison gang, the First Capital Command (PCC), obtain weapons in exchange for the protection of prisoners of Lebanese origin detained in Brazil.[54] The same reports indicated that Lebanese traffickers tied to Hezbollah reportedly helped sell C4 explosives that the PCC allegedly stole in Paraguay.[55]

Nor is Hezbollah plotting strictly an Israeli concern. "Beyond its role in Syria," Matt Olsen, the then-director of the National Counterterrorism Center (NCTC) warned in September 2014, "Lebanese Hezbollah remains committed to conducting terrorist activities worldwide." The NCTC director continued: "We remain concerned the group's activities could either endanger or target U.S. and other Western interests." NCTC officials note that Hezbollah "has engaged in an aggressive terrorist campaign in recent years and continues attack planning abroad."[56] Indeed, of the group's most recently foiled plots, one was in Peru—involving a Hezbollah operative married to a U.S. citizen.

Peruvian counterterrorism police arrested a Hezbollah operative in Lima in November 2014, the result of a surveillance operation that began several months earlier. In that case, Mohammed Amadar, a Lebanese citizen, arrived in Peru in November 2013 and married a dual Peruvian-American citizen two weeks later. They soon moved to Brazil, living in Sao Paulo until they returned to Lima in July 2014. Authorities were clearly aware of Amadar at the time, because they questioned him on arrival at the airport and began watching him then. When he was arrested in October, police raided his home and found traces of TNT, detonators, and other inflammable substances. A search of the garbage outside his home found chemicals used to manufacture explosives.[57] By the time of his arrest, intelligence indicated Amadar's targets included places associated with Israelis and Jews in Peru, including areas popular with Israeli backpackers, the Israeli embassy in Lima, and Jewish community institutions.

It warrants noting that Hezbollah activity in the Southern Hemisphere often includes links to the United States. This was underscored in January 2015 when the FBI's Miami field office released a "request for information" bulletin about a dual Venezuelan-Lebanese Hezbollah operative known both for raising money for the group and meeting with Hezbollah officials in Lebanon to discuss "operational issues."[58]

Hezbollah today is more invested in operations in South America than ever before. Not only are counterterrorism officials tracking Hezbollah operational plotlines there on a regular basis, but one of the most prominent operatives behind the AMIA bombing has now risen up the ranks of the organization and is personally overseeing Hezbollah operations in the region.[59]

Salman al-Reda, whose true name is reportedly Salman Raouf Salman, was the on-the-ground coordinator of the AMIA bombing. A dual Lebanese-Colombian citizen who lived at various times in Colombia, in Buenos Aires and in the Tri-Border area, al-Reda fled the region after the bombing, before being indicted by Argentine authorities for his role in the attack. But in the years that followed, he served as an active member of Hezbollah's Islamic Jihad Organization (IJO), the group's international terrorist apparatus, also known as the External Security Organization (ESO). He was especially active in Southeast Asia and South America in the 1990s, including a flurry of operational missions in 1997 with three visits to Panama, two to Colombia, and one to Brazil.[60] Following Mohammad Hamdar's arrest in Peru, he identified al-Reda as the Hezbollah operative who served as his handler and with whom he met with on three different occasions in Turkey to plan the Peru operation.[61]

Conclusion

Despite the Iran deal, or perhaps because of it, Hezbollah continues to present a significant threat to United States interests both in the Middle East and, as events in Europe and South America indicate, closer to home.

Iran is Hezbollah's primary benefactor, giving the Lebanese political party and militant group some $200 million a year in addition to weapons, training, intelligence, and logistical assistance. For about eighteen months prior to the Iran deal, however, Iran had cut back its financial support to Hezbollah -- a collateral benefit of the unprecedented international sanctions regime targeting Iran's nuclear program, as well as the fall in oil prices.

The cutback mostly curtailed Hezbollah's political, social, and military activities inside Lebanon. Its social-service institutions had to cut costs, employees received paychecks late or were laid off, and funding for civilian organizations, such as the group's satellite television station, al-Manar, had been reduced. By contrast, Hezbollah's Syria command, which has been a priority for Tehran given its commitment to defending Bashar al-Assad's regime, showed no sign of financial hardship even then.

Increased Iranian spending in the wake of the Iran deal is likely to benefit Hezbollah's regional and international operations. The group is no longer limited to jockeying for political power in Lebanon and fighting Israel. With more money, it should be expected to step up its aid to Shia militias in Iraq and Yemen in cooperation with Iran, sending small numbers of skilled trainers to bolster local forces and, in some cases, fight alongside them. In Iraq, Hezbollah is training and fighting with Shia militias, and that will likely expand. Though they are fighting on behalf of the government, their tactics exacerbate sectarian tensions. Hezbollah's footprint in Yemen is small, but it could expand with additional resources. Hezbollah is already trying to find long-term support for these operations, such as the investment in commercial front organizations in Iraq.

Finally, increased funding could help Hezbollah reconstitute its capabilities beyond the Middle East as well. Hezbollah is busier than ever, especially in Syria, where it is engaged in expensive militant operations and support activities. Meanwhile, the group has expanded its regional activities further afield, straining its coffers even as it has had to cut back its activities in Lebanon. A newly enriched Hezbollah should be expected to be more aggressive at home and abroad, challenging less-militant parties across the Lebanese political spectrum and boosting its destabilizing activities outside of Lebanon. And at a time when Iran may not want to be seen engaging directly in activities that could undermine the Iran deal, the likelihood increases that it will rely still more on the reasonably deniable activities of its primary terrorist proxy organization, Hezbollah.

The good news is that U.S. law enforcement has been proactively targeting Hezbollah criminal activities worldwide. Working closely with law enforcement agencies, the Treasury Department has not only picked up the pace of its Hezbollah designations but it has taken the financial fight to Beirut, where Hezbollah has until recently banked with impunity. Now armed with the Hezbollah International Financing Prevention Act, U.S. agencies truly are empowered to "thwart" the group's "network at every turn" by imposing sanctions on financial institutions that deal with Hezbollah or its al Manar television station.[62]

At the same time, through the Counterterrorism Partnership Fund (CTPF) the State Department has launched an international initiative to raise awareness about Iran and Hezbollah's broad range of terrorist and criminal activities around the world, and to increase law enforcement cooperation and coordination among a wide range of countries to counter these activities. The U.S. co-led the Law Enforcement Coordination Group with Europol focused on Hezbollah's illicit activities, and regional capacity building workshops were help in South America, Eastern Europe, West Africa, Southeast Asia all focused on improving local countries' ability to detect and prosecute Hezbollah's terrorist and criminal activities in their regions.

And Hezbollah has taken notice. Hezbollah leader Hassan Nasrallah gave lengthy televised addresses in July and December 2015, focused not on Hezbollah's battlefield losses in Syria but on denying that Hezbollah engages in commercial activities and declaring "unjust" charges that Hezbollah has ties to drug trafficking and money laundering. The vehement denials were a response to intensifying efforts by the U.S. and key allies to target Hezbollah's wide-ranging international organized criminal activities.[63]

Nasrallah further lamented that when the U.S. accuses people or businesses of having ties to Hezbollah, Lebanese banks actually "take measures" against those people or the accounts of their entities. Investigators have pursued so many Hezbollah-related cases in recent years that the group can no longer pretend to ignore them. The trail has led to the inner circle of Hezbollah's leadership, including Abdullah Safieddine, the group's representative to Iran and a cousin of Mr. Nasrallah.

In his December speech, Mr. Nasrallah challenged his accusers: "Bring me the evidence!" The U.S. and partner countries are doing just that, with great effect.

---

[1] Suleiman al Khalidi. "Lebanon's Hezbollah Leader Says Iran will not Abandon Support after Nuclear Deal," Reuters, July 25, 2015 http://www.reuters.com/article/us-lebanon-hezbollah-idUSKCN0PZ0LL20150725

[2] Hassan Nasrallah, "Interview of Hassan Nasrallah with Al-Ikhbariya Al-Soriya " (Arabic), Interview by Rania al-Dhanoun, Al-Ikhbariya Al-Soriya. April 6, 2015. http://alikhbariya.sy/index.php?d=1&id=1073

[3] Ali Rizk. "What Hezbollah stands to gain from Iran's nuclear deal," Al Monitor, February 16, 2016, http://www.al-monitor.com/pulse/originals/2016/02/iran-nuclear-deal-hezbollah-support.html#ixzz436236gcT

[4] Avi Issacharoff, "A third of Hezbollah's fighters said killed or injured in Syria," Times of Israel, December 15, 2015, http://www.timesofisrael.com/a-third-of-hezbollahs-fighters-said-killed-or-injured-in-syria/

[5] Laila Bassam, "Assad allies, including Iranians, prepare ground attack in Syria: sources," Reuters, October 1, 2015, http://www.reuters.com/article/us-mideast-crisis-syria-iranians-exclusi-idUSKCN0RV4DN20151001

[6] Erika Solomon, "Lebanon's Hizbollah and Yemen's Houthis open up on links," Financial Times, May 8, 2015, http://www.ft.com/cms/s/0/c1c6f750-f49b-11c4-9a58-00144fcab7dc.html#axzz4363W59gM

[7] "Top Commander: Declaring Hezbollah Terror Group Won't Affect Resistance's Position<" Fars News Agency, March 6, 2016, http://en.farsnews.com/newstext.aspx?nn=13941216000536

[8] "Iran Judiciary Chief Condemns Anti-Hezbollah Campaign," Fars News Agency, March 7, 2016, http://en.farsnews.com/print.aspx?nn=13941217001117

[9] Sultan al-Tamimi, "GCC: Hezbollah terror group," Arab News, June 3, 2013, http://www.arabnews.com/news/453834

[10] Fahd Al-Zayabi, "Saudi Arabia launches financial sanctions on Hezbollah," Asharq Al-Awsat, May 29, 2014, http://english.aawsat.com/2014/05/article55332700

[11] "Gulf Arab States Designate Hezbollah a Terrorist Organization," , March 2, 2016, http://english.aawsat.com/2016/03/article55348066/gulf-arab-states-designate-hezbollah-a-terrorist-organization

[12] Ben Hubbard, "Saudis Cut Off Funding for Military Aid to Lebanon," New York Times, February 19, 2016, http://www.nytimes.com/2016/02/20/world/middleeast/saudis-cut-off-funding-for-military-aid-to-lebanon.html?_r=0

[13] Terrorism Review October 22, 1987, CIA FOIA, http://www.foia.cia.gov/sites/default/files/document_conversions/89801/DOC_0000259360.pdf

[14] Matthew Levitt. "Iran and Bahrain: Crying Wolf, or Wolf at the Door?," The Washington Institute for Near East Policy, May 16, 2014, http://www.washingtoninstitute.org/policy-analysis/view/iran-and-bahrain-crying-wolf-or-wolf-at-the-door

[15] Matthew Levitt, "Iran and Bahrain: Crying Wolf, or Wolf at the Door?," The Washington Institute for Near East Policy, May 16, 2014, http://www.washingtoninstitute.org/policy-analysis/view/iran-and-bahrain-crying-wolf-or-wolf-at-the-door

[16] Matthew Levitt, "Iranian and Hezbollah Threats to Saudi Arabia: Past Precedents," *The Washington Institute for Near East Policy*, May 19, 2015, http://www.washingtoninstitute.org/policy-analysis/view/iranian-and-hezbollah-threats-to-saudi-arabia-past-precedents

[17] United States of America v. Ahmed al-Mughassil (Khobar Indictment). United States District Court Eastern District of Virginia Alexandria Division, June 2001, http://nsarchive.gwu.edu/NSAEBB/NSAEBB318/doc05.pdf
[18] Matthew Levitt, "29 Years Later, Echoes of "Kuwait 17," *Weekly Standard*, December 13, 2012, http://www.washingtoninstitute.org/policy-analysis/view/29-years-later-echoes-of-kuwait-17

[19] Nadav Pollak & Matthew Levitt, "Hezbollah in Iraq: A Little Help Can Go a Long Way," *The Washington Institute for Near East Policy*, June 25, 2014, http://www.washingtoninstitute.org/policy-analysis/view/hezbollah-in-iraq-a-little-help-can-go-a-long-way
[20] "Dubai Deputy Police Chief Says Hizbullah Trained Bahraini Bomb Attacker, Party Denies." *Naharnet*, March 4, 2014, http://www.naharnet.com/stories/en/121113-dubai-police-chief-says-hizbullah-trained-bahraini-bomb-attacker
[21] "Kuwait charges 'terror cell tied to Iran and Hezbollah'," *Al Jazeera*, September 1, 2015, http://www.aljazeera.com/news/2015/09/kuwait-charges-terror-cell-tied-iran-hezbollah-150901134517950.html
[22] Caline Malek, "Bahrain smashes 'Iran-linked' terror cell," *The National*, January 7, 2016, http://www.thenational.ae/world/middle-east/bahrain-smashes-iran-linked-terror-cell
[23] "UAE tries 'Hezbollah'. 'Qaeda' cell members: media," *DailyStar Lebanon*, February 9, 2016, http://www.dailystar.com.lb/News/Middle-East/2016/Feb-09/336357-uae-tries-hezbollah-qaeda-cell-members-media.ashx
[24] "Kuwait blacklists Hezbollah-linked journalists," *Kuwait Times*, March 17, 2016, http://news.kuwaittimes.net/website/kuwait-blacklists-hezbollah-linked-journalists/

[25] "Kuwait ups measures against Hezbollah-linked individuals," *DailyStar Lebanon*, March 17, 2016, http://www.dailystar.com.lb/News/Lebanon-News/2016/Mar-17/342700-kuwait-ups-measures-against-hezbollah-linked-individuals.ashx
[26] "Treasury Sanctions Hizballah Front Companies and Facilitators in Lebanon And Iraq," US Department of Treasury, June 10, 2015, https://www.treasury.gov/press-center/press-releases/Pages/jl0069.aspx
[27] "Saudi Arabia blacklists four firms, three Lebanese men over Hezbollah ties," *Reuters*, February 26, 2016, http://www.reuters.com/article/us-mideast-crisis-saudi-lebanon-idUSKCN0VZ1C2
[28] "Treasury Sanctions Hizballah Procurement Agents and Their Companies," US Department of Treasury, November 5, 2015, https://www.treasury.gov/press-center/press-releases/Pages/jl0255.aspx
[29] Nabih Bulos, "Who was Sheik Nimr al-Nimr? A look at the man whose execution rocked the Mideast," *LA Times*, January 5, 2016, http://www.latimes.com/world/middleeast/la-fg-sheik-nimr-profile-20160105-story.html; Ben Hubbard, " Iranian Protesters Ransack Saudi Embassy After Execution of Shiite Cleric." *New York Times*. January 2, 2016, http://www.nytimes.com/2016/01/03/world/middleeast/saudi-arabia-executes-47-sheikh-nimr-shiite-cleric.html
[30] Anne Barnard, "Saudi Arabia Cuts Billions in Aid to Lebanon, Opening Door for Iran," *New York Times*, March 2, 2016, http://www.nytimes.com/2016/03/03/world/middleeast/saudi-arabia-cuts-billions-in-aid-to-lebanon-opening-door-for-iran.html
[31] "Saudi Arabia, Gulf allies raise Lebanon travel warning amid Iran row," *Reuters*. February 23, 2016. http://www.reuters.com/article/us-saudi-lebanon-travel-idUSKCN0VW1L4
[32] "Nasrallah: Hezbollah sent fighters to Iraq," *DailyStar Lebanon*, March 7, 2016, https://www.dailystar.com.lb/News/Lebanon-News/2016/Mar-07/340892-nasrallah-hezbollah-sent-fighters-to-iraq.ashx
[33] Loveday Morris and Hugh Naylor, "Arab states fear nuclear deal will give Iran a bigger regional role," *Washington Post*, July 14, 2015, https://www.washingtonpost.com/world/middle_east/arab-states-fear-dangerous-iranian-nuclear-deal-will-shake-up-region/2015/07/14/96d68ff3-7fee-4bf5-9170-6bcc9dfc46aa_story.html; Michael Eisenstadt, Simon Henderson, Michael Knights, Matthew Levitt, and Andrew J. Tabler, "The Regional Impact of Additional Iranian Money," *The Washington Institute for Near East Policy*, July 28, 2015, http://www.washingtoninstitute.org/policy-analysis/view/the-regional-impact-of-additional-iranian-money

[34] Philip Smyth, "How Iran Is Building Its Syrian Hezbollah," *The Washington Institute for Near East Policy*, March 8, 2016, https://www.washingtoninstitute.org/policy-analysis/view/how-iran-is-building-its-syrian-hezbollah

21

[35] Philip Smyth, "How Iran Is Building Its Syrian Hezbollah," *The Washington Institute for Near East Policy*, March 8, 2016, https://www.washingtoninstitute.org/policy-analysis/view/how-iran-is-building-its-syrian-hezbollah
[36] "Nasrallah: Hezbollah sent fighters to Iraq," *DailyStar Lebanon*, March 7, 2016, https://www.dailystar.com.lb/News/Lebanon-News/2016/Mar-07/340892-nasrallah-hezbollah-sent-fighters-to-iraq.ashx
[37] "Treasury Sanctions Hizballah Front Companies and Facilitators in Lebanon And Iraq," US Department of Treasury, June 10, 2015, https://www.treasury.gov/press-center/press-releases/Pages/jl0069.aspx
[38] "Yemen government says Hezbollah fighting alongside Houthis," *Reuters*, February 24, 2016, http://www.reuters.com/article/us-yemen-security-idUSKCN0VX21N
[39] "Treasury Sanctions Hizballah Leadership," US Department of Treasury, August 22, 2013, https://www.treasury.gov/press-center/press-releases/Pages/jl2147.aspx

[40] Matthew Levitt, "Waking Up the Neighbors," *Foreign Affairs*, July 28, 2015, https://www.foreignaffairs.com/articles/israel/2015-07-23/waking-neighbors
[41] William Maclean, "Weapons bound for Yemen seized on Iranian boat: coalition," *Reuters*, September 30, 2015, http://www.reuters.com/article/us-yemen-security-idUSKCN0RU0R220150930
[42] "DEA and European Authorities Uncover Massive Hizballah Drug and Money Laundering Scheme," US Drug Enforcement Administration, February 1, 2016, http://www.dea.gov/divisions/hq/2016/hq020116.shtml
[43] "DEA and European Authorities Uncover Massive Hizballah Drug and Money Laundering Scheme," US Drug Enforcement Administration, February 1, 2016, http://www.dea.gov/divisions/hq/2016/hq020116.shtml
[44] "Treasury Sanctions Key Hizballah Money Laundering Network," US Department of Treasury, January 28, 2016, https://www.treasury.gov/press-center/press-releases/Pages/jl0331.aspx
[45] "Treasury Sanctions Hizballah Procurement Agents and Their Companies," US Department of Treasury, November 5, 2015, https://www.treasury.gov/press-center/press-releases/Pages/jl0255.aspx
[46] "Treasury Sanctions Hizballah Procurement Agents and Their Companies," US Department of Treasury, November 5, 2015, https://www.treasury.gov/press-center/press-releases/Pages/jl0255.aspx
[47] "Two Hezbollah Associates Arrested On Charges Of Conspiring To Launder Narcotics Proceeds And International Arms Trafficking," US Attorney's Office Eastern District of New York, October 9, 2015, https://www.justice.gov/usao-edny/pr/two-hezbollah-associates-arrested-charges-conspiring-launder-narcotics-proceeds-and

[48] "Two Hezbollah Associates Arrested On Charges Of Conspiring To Launder Narcotics Proceeds And International Arms Trafficking," US Attorney's Office Eastern District of New York, October 9, 2015, https://www.justice.gov/usao-edny/pr/two-hezbollah-associates-arrested-charges-conspiring-launder-narcotics-proceeds-and
[49] "Bulgaria identifies bomber of Israeli tourist bus," *Times of Israel*, July 18, 2014. http://www.timesofisrael.com/bulgaria-identifies-bomber-of-israeli-tourist-bus/
[50] Menelaos Hadjicostis, "Hezbollah member pleads guilty to 8 charges in Cyprus," *AP*, June 29, 2015, http://bigstory.ap.org/article/9b2fba18477b4f9098dd3da95fb0ff2b/hezbollah-member-pleads-guilty-8-charges-cyprus
[51] Matthew Levitt, "Inside Hezbollah's European Plots," *Daily Beast*, July 20, 2015, http://www.thedailybeast.com/articles/2015/07/20/inside-hezbollah-s-european-plots.html
[52] Menelaous Hadjicostas, "Israel Says Iran Building Terror Network in Europe, US," AP, February 24, 2016, http://bigstory.ap.org/article/32958bc6d5ee48c9bd18dd4dfc558d91/israel-says-iran-building-terror-network-europe-us
[53] "Hezbollah has ties to Brazil's Largest Criminal Gang; Group also Found Active in Peru," Fox News Latino, November 11, 2014. http://latino.foxnews.com/latino/news/2014/11/11/hezbollah-has-ties-to-brazil-largest-criminal-gang-group-also-found-active-in/
[54] "Hezbollah has ties to Brazil's Largest Criminal Gang; Group also Found Active in Peru," Fox News Latino, November 11, 2014. http://latino.foxnews.com/latino/news/2014/11/11/hezbollah-has-ties-to-brazil-largest-criminal-gang-group-also-found-active-in/
[55] "Hezbollah has ties to Brazil's Largest Criminal Gang; Group also Found Active in Peru," Fox News Latino, November 11, 2014. http://latino.foxnews.com/latino/news/2014/11/11/hezbollah-has-ties-to-brazil-largest-criminal-gang-group-also-found-active-in/

[56] Matthew G. Olsen, "Worldwide Threats to the Homeland," Hearing before the Senate Committee on Homeland Security, September 17, 2014. http://www.nctc.gov/docs/2014_worldwide_threats_to_the_homeland.pdf

[57] Stuart Winer, "Hezbollah operative targeted Jews, Israelis in Peru," *Times of Israel*, October 30, 2014, http://www.timesofisrael.com/hezbollah-operative-targeted-jews-israelis-in-peru/

[58] Federal Bureau of Investigation, Miami and San Diego Field Offices. "Seeking Information Ghazi Nasr al-Din," January 29, 2015, https://www.fbi.gov/wanted/terrorinfo/ghazi-nasr-al-din

[59] Author interview with counterterrorism officials, June 9, 2015

[60] Author interview with counterterrorism officials, June 9, 2015

[61] Author interview with counterterrorism officials, June 9, 2015

[62] "Statement by the Press Secretary on the Hizballah International Financing Prevention Act of 2015," December 18, 2015, https://www.whitehouse.gov/the-press-office/2015/12/18/statement-press-secretary-hizballah-international-financing-prevention

[63] "Nasrallah Says Hizbullah to Avenge Quntar at 'Appropriate Time, Place'," *Naharnet*, December 21, 2015, http://www.naharnet.com/stories/en/197665

Ms. ROS-LEHTINEN. We'll make sure that we ask you that. Thank you.

Mr. Badran.

STATEMENT OF MR. TONY BADRAN, RESEARCH FELLOW, FOUNDATION FOR DEFENSE OF DEMOCRACIES

Mr. BADRAN. Thank you, Madam Chair, and thank you, Ranking Member Deutch and for the members of the committee for allowing me to testify today.

I'm going to just briefly talk about, as Matt has talked about, Hezbollah's global operations. I want to talk specifically more about how that relates to their position in Lebanon and Syria specifically.

On the one hand, the Syrian uprising 5 years ago posed a significant challenge to Iran and Hezbollah by—as you noted, by threatening to sever their bridge to Lebanon and thereby denying Hezbollah their strategic depth as well as their logistical pipeline.

Unfortunately, 5 years on the trend is moving in the opposite direction. Hezbollah and Iran have secured their core interests in Syria, albeit at significant cost.

They have managed to secure contiguity between Lebanon and the regime-controlled areas in western Syria, thereby securing the ability to continue to move weapons from Damascus to Lebanon.

A key partner in this effort has been the Lebanese Armed Forces. In fact, one of the interesting things to note and troubling things to note over the past 5 years has been the growing partnership between Hezbollah and the LAF, which has allowed Hezbollah to protect its domestic flank when it was facing some backlash for its involvement in Syria.

The partnership between Hezbollah and the LAF, however, is not the only point of Hezbollah control and domination of the Lebanese state.

It has placed its members or sympathizers in key government positions which like, for instance, the Lebanese customs office as well as its financial auditor which allows it all this activity that we're hearing about globally to be processed domestically with little oversight or backlash.

In fact, Lebanon has become a critical hub in Hezbollah's criminal activities. Hezbollah has made Lebanon complicit both financially and economically as well as militarily because of all the weapons that it's moving from Syria that it's getting from Iran and is storing the majority of it in civilian areas.

Hezbollah has essentially painted a big target on the back of all of Lebanon and this is, unfortunately, has not been countered by U.S. policy over the last 5 years.

What this threatens to do is to—in addition to all these strategic weapons that are being moved to Lebanon as well as the Hezbollah's entrenchment in Syria and its expansion into the Golan along with the IRGC and the building of new infrastructure on Syrian soil, it creates a situation for Israel that will, I think, accelerate an upcoming future conflict which, as the IDF has been saying to anybody who will listen for the last few years, is going to be far bloodier than anything that we've ever seen on both sides.

You talked about the 4,000 rockets that they launched in the previous war. Now they have the capacity to launch anywhere between 1,000 to 1,500 a day.

So the IDF is very clear that there's going to be a lot of dead civilians both in Israel but also in Lebanon. The problem also has been that Hezbollah has gained operational expertise in Syria, working alongside the Russian military in combined weapons operations and in different urban and rural settings. So it's actually be able to offset its losses with this experience.

All of this creates a situation on the border of Israel in the northern border that now combines the Syrian front as well as the Lebanese front and soon to be not just swimming in Iranian cash but also potentially soon with an Iranian nuclear umbrella. This creates an unacceptable position for Israel.

But it's not only Israel's security that has been challenged by this development. It's also the Arab states and we've seen the Saudis leading the charge in this regard in designating Hezbollah but also in pulling the $3 billion aid that they gave to the Lebanese Armed Forces, citing the fact that the Lebanese Armed Forces have become an ''auxiliary'' of Hezbollah and I think this is an accurate assessment.

And although the—there's a tendency on the part of the administration at least to kind of pressure the Saudis to go back on that decision, I think actually we should stop and take and pause and reassess what exactly U.S. materiel support to the LAF and intelligence sharing—how that can actually go to sustain and help Hezbollah entrench its grip on Lebanon.

In addition, we should not—because of—the nature of Hezbollah's control over Lebanon—think about it in the way that the IRGC is in Iran. It's tentacles are everywhere in the economy and security apparatus.

So when pushing for the implementation of H.R. 2297, I think we should be very, very clear about not being taken hostage by the prospect that this is going to somehow collapse Lebanon's economy or the assistance to the LAF is going to collapse Lebanon's security, we have to also be cognizant of the fact that any nook and cranny and any safe haven that's provided in the Lebanese system ultimately is going to benefit Hezbollah because of its dominant position in the state, both in the security sector as well as in the economic sector.

So I'll stop right here and I'll be happy to flesh this out in the conversation.

[The prepared statement of Mr. Badran follows:]

Congressional Testimony

Hezbollah's Growing Threat Against U.S. National Security Interests in the Middle East

Tony Badran
Research Fellow
Foundation for Defense of Democracies

Hearing before House Foreign Affairs Committee
Subcommittee on Middle East and North Africa

Washington, DC
March 22, 2016

FOUNDATION FOR
DEFENSE OF DEMOCRACIES

1800 M Street NW • Suite 800, South Tower • Washington, DC 20036

Tony Badran   March 22, 2016

Chair Ros-Lehtinen, Ranking Member Deutch, I'd like to thank you for the opportunity to testify before the Middle East and North Africa Subcommittee.

The Syrian uprising constitutes one of the greatest challenges that Iran and Hezbollah have faced in decades. The collapse of the Assad regime would have, in the words of then-Commander of U.S. Central Command General James Mattis, dealt Iran "the biggest strategic setback in 25 years." It would have cut Iran's only land bridge to Lebanon, and deprived Hezbollah of its strategic depth.

Unfortunately, the situation in Syria has resulted in the opposite effect. While many, perhaps most, observers have tended to view Syria as a bloody quagmire that will erode Iranian ambitions, Tehran has deftly exploited the conflict, turning the strategic challenge it faces into an opportunity to expand its influence throughout the region.

In doing so, Iran has followed a well-developed template. It is building up Shiite militias, which it recruits from around the Greater Middle East, on the model of Hezbollah. This means it places the militias under the operational command of the Iranian Revolutionary Guard Corps (IRGC), and demands from them full allegiance to the Iranian regional project. The template goes back to the earliest days of the Islamic Revolution, but in recent years Iran has expanded its use to an extent never-before seen, with the biggest growth being in Iraq. Hezbollah, however, is the crown jewel of this region-wide network, with nodes in Syria, the Arab Gulf states, and, of course, Yemen.

This is arguably the most significant and most under-appreciated development in the region over the past five years. Iran's expansionist drive, through its legion of Shiite militias based on the model of Hezbollah and often trained by the group, has not been opposed by the U.S. If anything, Washington has effectively acquiesced to it, viewing it as a means to affect a new regional "equilibrium."

This has forced traditional U.S. regional allies – from Israel to Saudi Arabia – to look for measures to try and stop this emerging shift in the regional balance of power, which directly impacts their national security interests.

Although the effects are region-wide, this Iranian strategy has played out most consequentially in Syria. Five years into the uprising against the Assad regime, Iran and Hezbollah have secured their core interests in Syria. Hezbollah has taken significant losses at the tactical level but those have been offset by significant gains: Hezbollah is now better equipped and more operationally experienced than ever before.

The first-order priority for Hezbollah and Iran was to secure Assad's rule in Damascus and Western Syria. Maintaining control over key real estate in order to ensure territorial contiguity with Lebanon was essential. In fact, the Iran-Assad-Hezbollah axis showed a willingness to forgo ancillary territory relatively early in the conflict in order to secure the corridor between what might be called Assadistan and Hezbollahstan. Specifically, Hezbollah and Iran were determined to hold the areas adjacent to Lebanon's eastern border and secure the routes to Damascus. This is essential for safeguarding arms transfers from Iran to Lebanon, as well as for

Tony Badran   March 22, 2016

protecting weapons storage depots on Syrian soil. Hezbollah is now reportedly also working to ethnically cleanse these areas.

The campaign to create the security corridor has ensured that Hezbollah's supply lines have remained open and uninterrupted. In fact, shipments into Lebanon from Syria may have even accelerated, and they may have included the transfer of certain strategic weapons systems that were kept on Syrian soil, as evident from the list of reported Israeli airstrikes over the last three years.

As part of its effort to secure the border, Hezbollah deepened its partnership with the Lebanese Armed Forces (LAF), whose cooperation has been vital – and not only on the Syrian front. As Hezbollah began to face backlash in the form of car bombs in Beirut over its involvement in Syria in 2013, it looked to the LAF for support in protecting its domestic flank.

The partnership between the LAF and Hezbollah has grown to such an extent that it is now meaningful to speak of the LAF as an auxiliary force in Hezbollah's war effort. Indeed, in explaining the recent decision by Saudi Arabia to pull its $3 billion grant to the LAF, Saudi columnist Abdul Rahman al-Rashed wrote, "Hezbollah has started to use the army as its auxiliary in the war against the Syrians, which protects its lines and borders."

In certain instances, LAF troops and Hezbollah forces have deployed troops jointly, such as during street battles with the followers of a minor Sunni cleric in Sidon in 2013. The LAF routinely raids Syrian refugee camps and Sunni cities in Lebanon, rounding up Sunni men and often detaining them without charges. In a number of cases, it has arrested defected Syrian officers in the Free Syrian Army, either handing them back to the Assad regime, or, in some cases, delivering them to Hezbollah, which then uses them in prisoner swaps with the Syrian rebels.

The LAF-Hezbollah synergy is broadly recognized in the region, with strategic implications that have been only dimly perceived in the United States. The Saudis, as I noted above, have reacted by withdrawing their aid to the LAF – and they are by no means alone. The Israelis have no choice to but expect that if war should break out between them and Hezbollah, the LAF will come to the direct aid of the latter. The Israel Defense Forces (IDF) have therefore warned that in the next war, they will certainly target the LAF. In contrast to the policies of Israel and Saudi Arabia, the U.S. is not making its aid to the LAF contingent on it severing its operational ties with Hezbollah – a policy which many in the Middle East see as facilitating the partnership between the two.

Hezbollah's influence in Lebanon is by no means limited to its partnership with the LAF. Hezbollah exploits the weak and dysfunctional Lebanese state in order to advance its interests. It exerts direct influence over, for example, the Lebanese customs authority and the financial auditor's office in order to protect its criminal enterprises, and uses Lebanese territory for the training of Shiite militias in the Iranian network. As Lebanon's Interior Minister observed earlier this month, Lebanon is now the IRGC's "external operations room for training and sending fighters all over the world." Through Hezbollah, Iran has made the Lebanese state complicit in its activities.

Tony Badran   March 22, 2016

In his address to the United Nations General Assembly last October, Israeli Prime Minister Benjamin Netanyahu revealed that despite Israel's interdiction efforts, and in violation of UNSCR 1701, Iran had managed to bring advanced weapons systems into Lebanon, specifically the Russian-made Yakhont anti-ship cruise missiles, SA-22 (Pantsyr-S1) air defense system, and precision-guided surface-to-surface missiles – which presumably includes the upgraded Iranian Fateh-110 missiles with integrated GPS navigation.[1]

The Yakhont and the precision-guided missiles pose serious threats to Israel because they are capable of hitting strategic installations and targets deep inside the country as well as offshore. These advanced systems are, of course, in addition to the estimated 100,000 rockets and missiles that Hezbollah has already stored in Lebanon – mainly in civilian areas. When one considers that Hezbollah has the capability to rain down 1,500 rockets a day on Israel, it becomes clear that civilian casualties in the next war will be much higher on both sides than in any of the previous wars.

IDF officers believe that Hezbollah has amassed valuable tactical experience in Syria. The military capabilities of the Syrian opposition do not compare to those of the IDF; nevertheless, Hezbollah's units are mastering the use of diverse weapons systems, in both urban and rural settings. Over the past year, this experience has included working together with the Russian military, which has introduced new weapons systems and combined arms operations to the Syrian theater. In fact, Hezbollah, Iranian, and Russian officers have worked together on planning operations, and a joint operations room was reportedly also established in Iraq last year.

Iran and Hezbollah clearly intend to leverage their success in Syria to change the balance of power with Israel. Specifically, they have set their sights on expanding into the Golan Heights, and on linking it to the south Lebanon front. They signaled the importance they attached to this effort by sending a group of high-ranking Iranian and Hezbollah officers on a mission to Quneitra in January 2015. The Israelis destroyed that particular group, but we can be certain that they will resume their push there at a later date.

Iran and Hezbollah have invested in local Syrian communities to create a Syrian franchise of Hezbollah. Besides developing Alawite militias, they have also invested in Syria's Shiite and Druze communities. The Druze, by virtue of their concentration in southern Syria, are particularly attractive as potential partners. Hezbollah has cultivated recruits from the Druze of Quneitra and has used them in a number of attacks in the Golan over the past couple of years. In addition to recruitment to Syrian Hezbollah or other Shiite militias in Quneitra, there have also been some efforts with the Druze of Suwayda province near the Jordanian border.

As a result, the IDF is preparing for offensive incursions by Hezbollah into northern Israel in the next conflict. For Israel, Hezbollah's use of Lebanon as an Iranian forward missile base, its expansion into Syria with an aim to link the Golan to Lebanon, and the prospect of this reality

---

[1] See the included annex, prepared by my colleagues Patrick Megahan and David Daoud for FDD's Military Edge project, for information regarding Hezbollah's estimated inventory of weapons and recent Israeli strikes against Hezbollah weapons shipments.

Tony Badran   March 22, 2016

soon getting an Iranian nuclear umbrella, creates an unacceptable situation which, under the right circumstances, could easily trigger a major conflict.

It is hardly surprising, then, that Israeli officials have been loudly voicing the position that any settlement in Syria cannot leave Iran and Hezbollah in a position of dominance, and certainly not anywhere near the Golan. Unfortunately, this position is directly at odds with current U.S. policy. President Obama has stated that any solution in Syria must respect and protect so-called Iranian "equities" in Syria. When one actually spells out what these "equities" are – namely preserving the Syrian bridge to Hezbollah in Lebanon – it becomes clear that U.S. policy in Syria inadvertently complicates Israel's security challenge.

It also complicates the challenges of other critical U.S. allies, such as Jordan and Saudi Arabia. Indeed, Hezbollah's expansion has also spurred a Saudi-led campaign targeting the group, culminating in its designation as a terrorist organization by the Gulf Cooperation Council and the Arab League. The Saudis have also announced measures to freeze the accounts of any citizen or expatriate suspected of belonging to or supporting Hezbollah. Supporters would be prosecuted, jailed, and deported. Bahrain and the United Arab Emirates have followed suit, deporting a number of Lebanese expatriates with connections to Hezbollah.

There is talk – or perhaps a threat – that the Saudis might go after not just Shiite supporters, but also Christian businessmen who support the group or are part of its financial schemes, and who are seen as weak links because of their financial interests in the Gulf. The potential impact of Saudi measures against Hezbollah could be significant if followed through. However, as noted earlier regarding Hezbollah's relationship with the LAF, the Saudis have come to recognize that the Lebanese state itself is in Hezbollah's grip.

This is a bleak picture, but there are steps that Congress can take to help steer U.S. policy in the right direction.

First, Congress should push the administration on the implementation of H.R. 2297, targeting Hezbollah's criminal and financial activities. It's important not to be dissuaded by the argument that pushing too hard would break Lebanon's economy. It is critical to realize that Hezbollah's position in the Lebanese state and economy increasingly resembles that of the IRGC in the Iranian state. Moreover, it would be worthwhile to use the Arab League and Gulf Cooperation Council designation of Hezbollah to encourage the European Union to follow their lead in designating all of Hezbollah as a terrorist organization.

Second, security assistance to the LAF should be, at a minimum, reviewed. Although the Obama administration is said to be unhappy with the Saudi decision to suspend its aid to the LAF, it is a sound decision and should push the U.S. to reconsider its own policies. The United States cannot, under the pretext of combating Sunni jihadism, align with Iranian assets and Iranian-dominated "state institutions." Using this pretext, the U.S. has looked the other way from, if not condoned, the partnership between the LAF and Hezbollah. The result has been that U.S. military support and intelligence sharing has helped Hezbollah, if only indirectly.

Tony Badran   March 22, 2016

Finally and more broadly, the United States must conduct comprehensive realignment in the Middle East away from Iran and back towards its traditional allies. The place to begin that realignment is Syria. Instead of pushing for an endgame in Syria which preserves so-called Iranian "equities," or which creates cantons that function as Iranian protectorates, the United States should be working with its allies to impose severe costs on Hezbollah for its Syrian adventure.

Obviously, the White House holds the keys to such a realignment, but Congress can certainly help. It can, for example, hold the administration to its promise to "push back" against Iranian regional expansionism. Our Israeli, Jordanian, and Saudi allies have voiced their deep concerns about how a Syrian endgame that leaves Iran entrenched in Syria threatens their security. The U.S. response should not be to tell them to "share the region" with Iran. Rather, it should be to help them roll back the threat posed by Iran and Hezbollah.

Appendix:

Hezbollah's Arsenal – March 2016

Prepared by Project on Military Edge:
A Project of the Foundation for Defense of Democracies

Indirect Fire Munitions/Long Range Rockets and Missiles

As of November 2015, the IDF assessed Hezbollah has a stockpile of 150,000 "rockets and missiles."[2] This is up from 100,000 estimated last May and five times the number believed to have been in their inventory in 2006 – of which nearly 4,000 rockets were fired into Israel.[3] The specifics to how the IDF classifies "rockets and missiles" is fairly broad and could range from short-range mortars to long range surface-to-surface guided ballistic missiles such as the Iranian-made Fateh-110. Indirect fire weapons that Hezbollah is believe to possess include:

- Mortars
    - 81mm – 4.9 km range; 4.05 kg warhead[4]
    - 120mm – 6 km range; 13 kg warhead[5]
- Unguided rockets
    - 107mm Type-63 – 8.5 km range; 5-7 kg warhead[6]

---

[2] Avi Issacharoff, "Israel raises Hezbollah rocket estimated to 150,000," *The Times of Israel*, November 12, 2015, (http://www.timesofisrael.com/israel-raises-hezbollah-rocket-estimate-to-150000/).
[3] "Hezbollah hiding 100,000 missiles that can hit north, army says," *The Associated Press*, May 13, 2015. (http://www.timesofisrael.com/hezbollah-hiding-100000-missiles-that-can-hit-north-army-says/); William M. Arkin, *Divining Victory: Airpower in the 2006 Israel-Hezbollah War*, (Maxwell Air Force Base: Air University Press, 2011), page 32. (https://books.google.com/books?id=Q-NiAwAAQBAJ&pg=PA32&lpg=PA32&dq=Falaq-2+hezbollah&source=bl&ots=pXYudkXcZT&sig=C6HFV727pWCsBO53n4DQDSNiB2Q&hl=en&sa=X&ei=6Paf VY2_MMcx-QHVopzoAg&ved=0CEIQ6AEwBg#v=onepage&q=Falaq-2%20hezbollah&f=false); "Middle East crisis: Facts and figures," *BBC* (UK), August 31, 2006. (http://news.bbc.co.uk/2/hi/middle_east/5257128.stm)
[4] Galen Wright, "Mortar Artillery," *The Arkenstone*, April 4, 2011. (http://thearkenstone.blogspot.com/2011/04/mortar-artillery.html)
[5] Galen Wright, "Mortar Artillery," *The Arkenstone*, April 4, 2011. (http://thearkenstone.blogspot.com/2011/04/mortar-artillery.html)

Tony Badran   March 22, 2016

- o   122mm Grad/Katyusha – 20-40 km range; 10-60 kg warhead[7]
- o   240mm Fajr 3 – 43 km range; 90 kg warhead[8]
- o   240mm Falaq-1 – 10 km range; 50 kg warhead[9]
- o   333mm Fajr 5 – 75 km range; 175 kg warhead[10]
- o   333mm Falaq-2 – 10 km range; 120 kg warhead[11]
- o   302mm Khaibar – 100-212 km range; 175 kg warhead[12]
- o   610mm Zelzal-2 – 250 km range; 600 kg warhead[13]
- Guided ballistic missiles*
  - o   Fateh-110/M600 – 200-300 km range; 500-650 kg warhead; Made by Iran and Syria[14]
  - o   Scud C – 600 km range; 600-700 kg warhead; Made by USSR, North Korea, China, Iran, and Syria[15]
  - o   Scud D – 700 km range; 500 kg warhead; North Korean-made; sold to Syria[16]

*Claimed, but never seen in Hezbollah's possession and difficult to conceal given their size.

As Hezbollah's most feared weapon, indirect fire munitions – such as unguided rockets, mortars, and guided missiles – carry significant benefit for a group which lacks the manpower and resources of its rivals. At low cost, Hezbollah has amassed a large amount of firepower that can be rapidly deployed and reach deep into Israeli territory. On the other hand, the rockets lack the accuracy of conventional artillery systems (only 23 percent landed in populated areas in 2006) and hold almost no tactical military advantage.[17] In part, Hezbollah is forced to stock large numbers of rockets to improve the chance of striking targets and overwhelming defensive systems like Iron Dome. But strategically, they allow the group to strike deep into Israeli territory, having a profound psychological impact without losing fighters on direct assaults into Israeli territory.

While cheap for Hezbollah, its rocket and missile arsenal place a substantial financial burden on Israel even before they fire a shot. To protect civilian and military infrastructure, Israel is forced to invest in

[6] *Jane's Weapon Systems*, 19th Edition, 1988-1989, (Coulsdon, United Kingdom: Jane's Information Group, 1988), page 116.
[7] Threat Support Directorate, U.S. Army Training and Doctrine Command, *OPFOR: Worldwide Equipment Guide*, (Ft. Leavenworth, KS, 1999), Page 125.
[8] Patrick Megahan, "240mm Fajr 3," *Military Edge*, January 2014. (http://militaryedge.org/armaments/fajr-3/)
[9] N.R. Jenzen-Jones, Yuri Lyamin, and Galen Wright, "Iranian Falaq-1 and Falaq-2 Rockets in Syria," ARES, May 2014. (http://www.armamentresearch.com/wp-content/uploads/2014/01/ARES-Research-Report-No.-2-Iranian-Falaq-1-Falaq-2-Rockets-in-Syria.pdf)
[10] Patrick Megahan, "333mm Fajr 5 (M-75)," *Military Edge*, January 2014. (http://militaryedge.org/armaments/fajr-5/)
[11] William M. Arkin, *Divining Victory: Airpower in the 2006 Israel-Hezbollah War*, (Maxwell Air Force Base: Air University Press, 2011), page 32. (https://books.google.com/books?id=Q-NiAwAAQBAJ&pg=PA32&lpg=PA32&dq=Falaq-2+hezbollah&source=bl&ots=pXYudkXcZT&sig=C6HFV727pWCsBO53n4DQDSNjB2Q&hl=en&sa=X&ei=6PafVY2_MMex-QHVopzoAg&ved=0CEIQ6AEwBg#v=onepage&q=Falaq-2%20hezbollah&f=false)
[12] Patrick Megahan, "302mm Khaibar (M-302)," *Military Edge*, March 2014. (http://militaryedge.org/armaments/302mm-khaibar/)
[13] Patrick Megahan, "610mm Zelzal-2," *Military Edge*, January 2014. (http://militaryedge.org/armaments/zelzal-2/)
[14] Patrick Megahan, "Fateh-110/M-600," *Military Edge*, January 2014. (http://militaryedge.org/armaments/fateh-110m600/)
[15] Charles P. Vick, "Hwasong 6 / Scud-C – North Korea," *Federation of American Scientists*, February 17, 2015. (http://fas.org/nuke/guide/dprk/missile/hwasong-6.htm)
[16] Jeremy Binnie, "IDF Corroborates Hizbullah 'Scud-D' Claims," *IHS Jane's 360*, March 2, 2015. (http://www.janes.com/article/49668/idf-corroborates-hizbullah-scud-d-claims)
[17] Benjamin S. Lambeth, *Air Operations in Israel's War Against Hezbollah*, (Santa Monica: Rand Corporation, 2011), page 145.

Tony Badran   March 22, 2016

expensive countermeasures (Iron Dome, Patriot, and David Sling) and the hardening of key facilities and infrastructure. And once they are put into action, the persistent bombardment on the Israeli homeland causes significant disruption of daily life and thus the nation's economy. In 2006, it is estimated that the sustained rocket attacks by Hezbollah cost the Israeli economy $5.5 billion.[18]

While the larger, longer-range projectiles are often cited for the need to invest heavily in missile defense, during the 2006 war, 95 percent of the 4,338 rockets that landed in Israel were classified as shorter-range Katyushas. In fact, much of the group's larger missile systems were quickly taken out by the Israel Air Force (as many as 60 percent in the first five days of the war), while their shorter-range rockets were able to maintain a sustained rate of fire of about 116 launches per day.[19] Because of their size, preparation to fire the larger missiles requires more time, exposing the crews to aerial surveillance which can quickly be used to target the system before a launch. It is unclear if Hezbollah fighters would be able to effectively utilize such weapons or rely on foreign advisors to launch, raising the potential risks to the group's sponsors (as has been the case in Syria and Iraq where senior Iranian officers have been killed).

Guided Anti-Tank Missiles

Beginning during the 2006 war in Lebanon, Hezbollah has dramatically increased the effectiveness of its ground units with the use of guided anti-tank missiles (ATGMs). In that conflict, the majority of IDF casualties reportedly came from the use of anti-tank missiles and rockets.[20] It is believed that ATGMs were used to even bring down a low-flying Israeli CH-53 helicopter during the ground invasion of southern Lebanon.[21] More recently, in the cross-border attack in January 2015, ATGMs were used to target an IDF border patrol, killing two and wounding seven.[22] The quantity of Hezbollah's ATGM inventory is unknown but estimates suggest several hundred missiles given the frequency of their use and the proliferation of such systems in neighboring Syria. ATGMs known to be in Hezbollah's arsenal include:

- AT-3 Sagger – 3,000 m range; wire-guided; introduced 1961; Soviet-made; sold to Iran, Libya, Syria[23]
- AT-4 Spigot – 2,000 m range; wire-guided; introduced 1972; Soviet-made; sold to Iran, Libya, Syria[24]
- AT-5 Spandrel – 4,000 m range; wire-guided; introduced 1977; Soviet-made (Iran produces a copy); sold to Syria and Turkey[25]
- Metis-M (AT-13) – 1,500 m range; wire-guided; introduced 1992; Russian-made; sold to Syria[26]

---

[18] Benjamin S. Lambeth, *Air Operations in Israel's War Against Hezbollah*, (Santa Monica: Rand Corporation, 2011), page 146.

[19] Benjamin S. Lambeth, *Air Operations in Israel's War Against Hezbollah*, (Santa Monica: Rand Corporation, 2011), page 145.

[20] Ze'ev Schiff, "Hezbollah anti-tank fire causing most IDF casualties in Lebanon," Haaretz, August 6, 2006. (http://www.haaretz.com/news/hezbollah-anti-tank-fire-causing-most-idf-casualties-in-lebanon-1.194528)

[21] Benjamin S. Lambeth, Air Operations in Israel's War Against Hezbollah, (Santa Monica: Rand Corporation, 2011), page 129.

[22] Jodi Rudoren and Anne Barnard, "Hezbollah Kills 2 Israeli Soldiers Near Lebanon," *The New York Times*, January 28, 2015. (http://www.nytimes.com/2015/01/29/world/middleeast/israel-lebanon-hezbollah-missile-attack.html?_r=0)

[23] Threat Support Directorate, U.S. Army Training and Doctrine Command, *OPFOR: Worldwide Equipment Guide*, (Ft. Leavenworth, KS, 1999), Page 103.

[24] Threat Support Directorate, U.S. Army Training and Doctrine Command, *OPFOR: Worldwide Equipment Guide*, (Ft. Leavenworth, KS, 1999), Page 104.

[25] Threat Support Directorate, U.S. Army Training and Doctrine Command, *OPFOR: Worldwide Equipment Guide*, (Ft. Leavenworth, KS, 1999), Page 104.

Tony Badran   March 22, 2016

- AT-14 Kornet – 5,000 m range; laser-guided; introduced 1994; Russian-made (Iran claims to produces a copy); sold to Syria and Turkey[27]
- Milan – 2,000 m range; wire-guided; introduced 1972; French-made; sold to Lebanon and Syria[28]
- TOW – 3,750 m range; wire-guided; introduced 1970; American-made (Iran produces a copy called the Toophan); sold to Iran (pre-1979), Turkey, Lebanon, Syrian rebels[29]

This list does not include unguided anti-tank rockets such as RPG-7s and RPG-29s which require firing at targets at closer ranges to be accurate and tend to be more abundant.

ATGMs, like indirect fire weapons, allow fighters to target adversaries at range but with increased accuracy and the ability to penetrate armor and hardened defenses. The development of active protective systems like Trophy allows IDF forces to neutralize incoming missiles when fired at vehicles. But, like saturated rocket attacks which could overwhelm systems like Iron Dome, volleys of ATGMs on a single vehicle equipped with Trophy could negate the system. Hezbollah has already demonstrated this tactic when targeting IDF convoys.

Anti-Ship Guided Missiles

In the 2006 war in Lebanon, Hezbollah caught the Israeli Navy by surprise when it launched two C-802 anti-ship missiles (AShMs) at an Israeli warship patrolling near the Lebanese coast. One of the missiles struck the Israeli ship, which did not deploy any countermeasures to thwart the attack, killing four sailors. Meanwhile, the second missile struck and sank a Cambodian merchant ship nearby.[30] Members of the IRGC-Quds Force are believed to have assisted in the launching of the missiles while Lebanese shore-based radar stations were allegedly used to locate the ship.[31] Since then, reports suggest advanced P-800 Yakhont AShMs were supplied by Syria to Hezbollah.[32] These missiles have more sophisticated guidance systems and reach supersonic speeds, making them harder to intercept. While these systems demonstrate some of the most sophisticated weapons in Hezbollah's arsenal, their numbers are believed to be fairly low.

- C-802 Saccade – 120 km range; Mach 0.9; Chinese-made, Iran copied and renamed the 'Noor'[33]
- P-800 Yakhont – 120 km range; Mach 1.7; Russian-made, sold to Syria[34]

---

[26] Threat Support Directorate, U.S. Army Training and Doctrine Command, *OPFOR: Worldwide Equipment Guide*, (Ft. Leavenworth, KS, 1999), Page 105.

[27] "Kornet (AT-14)," *Federation of American Scientists*, June 19, 1999. (http://fas.org/man/dod-101/sys/land/row/at-14.htm)

[28] *Jane's Weapon Systems*, 19th Edition, 1988-1989, (Coulsdon, United Kingdom: Jane's Information Group, 1988), page 142.

[29] "M-220 Tube-launched, Optically tracked, Wire-guided missile (TOW)," *Federation of American Scientists*, February 22, 2000. (http://fas.org/man/dod-101/sys/land/tow.htm)

[30] Mark Mazzetti and Thom Shanker, "Arming of Hezbollah Reveals U.S. and Israeli Blind Spots," *The New York Times*, July 19, 2006.
(http://www.nytimes.com/2006/07/19/world/middleeast/19missile.html?pagewanted=print&_r=0)

[31] William M. Arkin, *Divining Victory: Airpower in the 2006 Israel-Hezbollah War*, (Maxwell Air Force Base: Air University Press, 2011), page 94. (https://books.google.com/books?id=Q-NiAwAAQBAJ&pg=PA32&lpg=PA32&dq=Falaq-2+hezbollah&source=bl&ots=pXYudkXcZT&sig=C6HFV727pWCsBO53n4DQDSNjB2Q&hl=en&sa=X&ei=6PafVY2_MMex-QHVopzoAg&ved=0CEIQ6AEwBg#v=onepage&q=Falaq-2%20hezbollah&f=false)

[32] Patrick Megahan, "Russian Yakhont Missiles in Hezbollah's Hands," *Military Edge*, January 4, 2014. (http://militaryedge.org/analysis-articles/russian-yakhont-missiles-hezbollahs-hands/)

[33] "C-802 / YJ-2 / Ying Ji-802," *Federation of American Scientists*, February 17, 2000. (https://www.fas.org/man/dod-101/sys/missile/row/c-802.htm)

Tony Badran   March 22, 2016

Drones

Hezbollah first started acquired low-tech drones from Iran in 2002. In 2004, Hezbollah is first believed to have flown an Iranian-made Mirsad-1 drone into Israeli airspace, followed by a second flight in 2005. Both flights appeared to be unarmed reconnaissance missions which reached as far as 18 miles into Israel and evaded Israeli defenses. During the 2006 war, Hezbollah is believed to have flown three Iranian-produced Ababil-2 drones armed with 40-50 kilograms of explosives on board. Israeli aircraft managed to intercept them before they reached their targets. Two more drones are reported to have crossed into Israeli airspace, with one reaching as far as Dimona in southern Israel in 2012. Hezbollah has claimed to have sent armed drones into Syria to fight rebel groups there, but video of the alleged strikes appears questionable.[35]

Hezbollah's drones are principally used for surveillance and are typically not armed with any sophisticated guided weapons. If such drones did exist in the terror group's possession, they would have to be much larger than the unmanned aerial vehicles it has used in the past in order to support a heavily payload of missiles and targeting systems. However, reports suggest Iran is attempting to equip Hezbollah with smaller suicide drones.[36] This would allow the group to accurately reach targets deep inside Israel. Drones believed to currently be in Hezbollah's inventory include:

- Mirsad-1 (Mohajer-4) – 30 km estimated range; 6,500 ft max altitude; unarmed[37]
- Ababil-2 – 100 km range; 9,800 ft max altitude; optionally armed w/ 30kg warhead[38]
- Ayoub – 250 km estimated range; unknown max altitude; unarmed[39]

Surface-to-Air Missiles

Little is known about Hezbollah's arsenal of surface-to-air missile (SAM) systems since there is no confirmed reports of the group using them in combat. During the 2006 war, some Israeli helicopter crews did report attempts to down their aircraft by SA-18 man portable air defense systems, or MANPADS.[40] Nevertheless, Hezbollah and its supporters in Iran and Syria have made numerous efforts to smuggle missiles into Lebanon. It is likely that significant quantities of MANPADS have reached the terror group because of their small size and abundance in the region. Beyond the SA-18s, other systems likely include Russian-made SA-7s from Libya and Iranian copies of Chinese QW-1s.[41] These systems have relatively

[34] Patrick Megahan, "P-800 Yakhont (SS-N-26 Strobile)," *Military Edge*, January 2014. (http://militaryedge.org/armaments/p-800ss-n-26-yakhont/)
[35] "Watch: Hezbollah uses drones against Syrian rebels," *The Jerusalem Post* (Israel), September 21, 2014. (http://www.jpost.com/Middle-East/Watch-Hezbollah-uses-drones-against-Syrian-rebels-375986)
[36] "'Iran helping Hamas, Hezbollah build fleet of suicide drones,'" *The Jerusalem Post* (Israel), April 9, 2015. (http://www.jpost.com/Middle-East/Iran-helping-Hamas-Hezbollah-build-fleet-of-suicide-drones-396673)
[37] Milton Hoenig, "Hezbollah and the Use of Drones as a Weapon of Terrorism," *Federation of American Scientists*, June 5, 2014. (http://fas.org/pir-pubs/hezbollah-use-drones-weapon-terrorism/)
[38] Galen Wright, "Ababil UAV," *The Arkenstone*, February 5, 2011. (http://thearkenstone.blogspot.com/2011/02/ababil-uav.html)
[39] Milton Hoenig, "Hezbollah and the Use of Drones as a Weapon of Terrorism," *Federation of American Scientists*, June 5, 2014. (http://fas.org/pir-pubs/hezbollah-use-drones-weapon-terrorism/)
[40] Benjamin S. Lambeth, *Air Operations in Israel's War Against Hezbollah*, (Santa Monica: Rand Corporation, 2011), page 75.
[41] Michelle Nichols, "Shoulder-launched anti-aircraft missiles flow abroad from Libya: U.N.," *Reuters*, March 11, 2014. (http://www.reuters.com/article/2014/03/11/us-libya-crisis-un-idUSBREA2A1MY20140311); "Iran to send missiles to Hizbullah," *Ynet News* (Israel), August 6, 2006. (http://www.ynetnews.com/articles/0,7340,L-3286926,00.html)

Tony Badran   March 22, 2016

short ranges and are easily thwarted by modern countermeasures but do still pose a threat to low flying fixed-wing aircraft, drones, and helicopters.

Israel has been vigilant to prevent larger, more sophisticated systems from reaching Hezbollah from Syria. Multiple airstrikes have been conducted inside of Syria targeting weapon convoys believed destined for Hezbollah. SA-8 and SA-17 SAMs are believed to have been part of these convoys.[42] Both systems are highly mobile and would represent a significant threat to military and commercial aircraft as the downing of Malaysian Airlines flight 17 demonstrated in July 2014.

- SA-7 – 5,500 m range; 4,500 m max altitude; Infrared guided MANPADS; Soviet-made; sold to Libya, Sudan, Syria, and Iran[43]
- QW-1 – 5,000 m range; 4,000 m max altitude; infrared guided MANPADS; Chinese-made (Iran copied and renamed 'Misagh-1')[44]
- SA-18 – 5,200 m range; 3,500 m max altitude; infrared guided MANPADS; Russian-made; Sold to Syria[45]
- SA-8 – 15 km range; 12,000 m max altitude; radar guided; Soviet-made; sold to Syria[46]
- SA-17 – 50 km range; 25,000 m max altitude; radar guided; Soviet-made; sold to Syria[47]
- SA-22 (Pantsir S1) – 20 km range; 15,000 m max altitude; radar guided; Russian-made; sold to Syria[48]

Nevertheless, there are major challenges to using large sophisticated SAMs like the SA-8, SA-17, and potentially the newer SA-22, which would limit their use by Hezbollah in a future conflict. Specifically, this would include concealing such large equipment from Israeli surveillance and avoiding detection when in use. SAMs using radar become extremely vulnerable when turned on because the radar signal they emit can be detected by military aircraft which can then hone-in on the source. Hezbollah would have to employ methods similar to how it launches rockets, where they quickly break cover, fire, and relocate before retaliatory strikes occur. But unlike the low-tech rockets which utilize crude improvised launchers, the crew, radars, and launchers would need to survive return fire to be used again. Sufficient cover, such as multiple warehouses that the vehicles could relocate to for concealment, would be required.

Israeli Strikes in Syria

As the Syrian Civil War rages, Israel has conducted a number of sporadic strikes inside the war-torn country. These strikes are to enforce Israel's so-called "red line" in Syria, which includes transfers of sophisticated weapon systems to Hezbollah in Lebanon and threats along its border.

---

[42] Roi Kais, "US confirms: Israel attacked Syrian missile base," *Ynet News* (Israel), October 31, 2013. (http://www.ynetnews.com/articles/0,7340,L-4448123,00.html)

[43] Threat Support Directorate, U.S. Army Training and Doctrine Command, *OPFOR: Worldwide Equipment Guide*, (Ft. Leavenworth, KS, 1999), page 141.

[44] John Pike, "QW-1," *Federation of American Scientists*, August 10, 1999. (http://fas.org/man/dod-101/sys/missile/row/qw-1.htm)

[45] John Pike, "SA-18 Grouse," *Federation of American Scientists*. October 16, 1999. (http://fas.org/man/dod-101/sys/missile/row/sa-18.htm)

[46] "SA-8 Gecko," *Federation of American Scientists*, February 4, 2000. (http://fas.org/man/dod-101/sys/missile/row/sa-8.htm)

[47] Dr. Carlo Kopp, "NIIP 9K37/9K37M1/9K317 Buk M1/M2 Self Propelled Air Defence System / SA-11/17 Gadfly/Grizzly," *Air Power Australia*, July 2009. (http://www.ausairpower.net/APA-9K37-Buk.html)

[48] "Pantsir-S1," *KBP Instrument Design Bureau*, September 8, 2014. (http://www.kbptula.ru/en/productions/air-defense-weapon-systems/pantsir-s1)

Tony Badran   March 22, 2016

Below is a timeline of reported strikes inside Syria:[49]

- **February 17, 2016** – Jabal Al-Manea: Three missiles struck a Syrian Army munitions warehouse located near the road to Deraa. It's unclear whether the weapons targeted were meant for Hezbollah. No casualties are reported.

- **February 8, 2016** – 155th Brigade Missile Base: Israeli jets are believed to have struck Scud missile warehouses on the outskirts of Damascus – likely the 155th Brigade missile base. No casualties are reported.

- **December 19, 2015** – Jarmana: An apartment building housing mid-level Hezbollah operative Samir Quntar, who also reportedly served as a commander in the Popular Resistance Committees, is struck. Nine others are killed, including Farhan Al-Shaalan (commander of the Syrian Resistance to Liberate the Golan) and Taysir Al-Na'su.

- **December 4, 2015** – Al-Qutayfah: Hezbollah and Syrian Army positions, including a truck carrying a Scud missile at the 155th Brigade Base is targeted. No casualties are reported.

- **November 29, 2015** – Ra's Al-Ayn, Assal Al-Ward, and Al-Jibba: Hezbollah positions, observation points, and Kornet missile warehouses are targeted. An unknown number of Hezbollah fighters and Syrian soldiers were killed.

- **November 26, 2015** – Fleita: Three strikes on Hezbollah positions on hillside forcing a withdraw to Fleita. No casualties are reported.

- **November 24, 2015** – Qara, Ras Al-Ma'arah, and Fleita: Unspecified Hezbollah and Syrian regime positions were targeted. As many as eight Hezbollah fighters and five Syrian soldiers were killed, dozens wounded.

- **November 11, 2015** – Outskirts of Damascus International Airport: Hezbollah facility believed to be host offices and warehouses is targeted. No casualties are reported.

- **October 31, 2015** – Qalamoun Mountains: Two strikes on Hezbollah and Syrian army targets, including a weapons convoy destined for Hezbollah. No casualties are reported.

- **October 30, 2015** – Al-Qutayfah: Warehouses holding Scud missiles belonging to the 155th Brigade that were believed destined for Hezbollah is targeted. No casualties are reported.

- **October 30, 2015** – Ina'ash: A military installation believed to host Hezbollah is targeted. No casualties are reported.

- **August 20/21, 2015** – Al-Kawm: The Syrian Army's 90th Brigade's base is struck. Five soldiers or paramilitary fighters loyal to Assad as well as two others are killed. Israel claims four Palestinian members of Islamic Jihad were killed. Islamic Jihad denies it lost any members.

- **August 20/21, 2015** – Khan Al-Sheikh: The Syrian Army's 68th Brigade base is struck but the intended target is unknown. Five soldiers or paramilitary fighters loyal to Assad as well as two others are killed.

---

[49] David Daoud and Patrick Megahan, "Tracker: Israeli Strikes in Syria," *Military Edge*, February 18, 2016. (http://militaryedge.org/analysis-articles/tracker-israeli-strikes-syria/)

- **July 29, 2015** – Hader: A four-wheeled drive vehicle containing two Hezbollah members and three Syrians is targeted.

- **April 27, 2015** – Majdal Shams: Four Syrians attempting to plant IEDs by border fence are killed.

- **April 27, 2015** – 155th Brigade Missile Base: A missile base belonging to the 155th Brigade, which was believed to be transferring Scud missiles to Hezbollah, is targeted. Israel denied conducting the strike. An unknown number of unidentified dead and wound are reported.

- **April 25, 2015** – Qalamoun Mountains: An artillery and missile installation which contained mid-ranged missiles belonging to the Syrian Army's 155th and 65th Brigades is believed to have been targeted. No casualties are reported.

- **January 28, 2015** – Golan Heights: Syrian military outposts are targeted in response to rocket fire landing in the Israeli-controlled areas of the Golan Heights. No casualties are reported.

- **January 24/25, 2015** – Latakia: Sophisticated missile equipment, including Russian-made SA-3 (S-125 Pechora-2M) surface-to-air missiles believed destined for Hezbollah, is targeted. No casualties are reported.

- **January 18, 2015** – Mazraat Amal: A convoy carrying senior Hezbollah members and an IRGC general who were planning a cross-border attack on Israel is struck. Seven individuals were identified as being killed: "Jawad" Jihad Mughniyeh, field commander "Abu Issa" Mohammad Issa, "Sayyed Abbas" Abbas Ibrahim Hijazi, "Kazem" Mohammad Ali Hassan Abu Al Hassan, "Daniel" Ghazi Ali Dawi, "Ihab" Ali Hassan Ibrahim, and IRGC Brigadier General Momammad Ali Allahdadi. Some sources claimed six unidentified Iranians were also killed.

- **December 7, 2014** – Damascus International Airport: A military facility connected to the airport which serves as a depot for newly-arrived weapons is struck. Three Hezbollah members are believed killed.

- **December 7, 2014** – Al-Dimas: Weapons depots and hangars in and around a small airfield are targeted. Unclear if weapons belong to Syrian government or Hezbollah. Three Hezbollah members are believed killed.

- **July 15, 2014** – Baath City: Three strikes in the Quneitra area hit a Syrian military base belonging to the 90th Brigade and several other army posts. Between four and 12 people are killed.

- **June 22/23, 2014** – Quneitra: Nine Syrian military positions, including the headquarters of the 90th Brigade, two tanks, and an artillery position, are targeted in response to an attack killing Israeli-Arab child. Ten Syrian soldiers are believed killed.

- **March 19, 2014** – Nouriyeh: A Syrian Army headquarters, artillery batteries, and a training camp are targeted in response to a roadside bomb attack on IDF vehicle. Syrian Army claims one soldier was killed, seven wounded.

Tony Badran   March 22, 2016

- **February 25, 2014** – Yabroud, Zabadani, and Qalamoun: A Hezbollah artillery position was targeted. Five members of Hezbollah, including group commander Abu Jamil Younes, are believed killed.

- **February 24, 2014** – Nabi Sheet: A suspected Hezbollah "missile base" or weapons convoy carrying unspecified missiles across the border is targeted. Several Hezbollah fighters are killed.

- **October 31/November 1, 2013** – Jableh: Sophisticated missile equipment, including Russian-made SA-3 (S-125 Pechora-2M) surface-to-air missiles believed destined for Hezbollah, is targeted. No casualties are reported.

- **October 30, 2013** – Ain Shikak: A strategic missile battery housing unspecified long-range Russian-made missiles or a shipment of SA-8 (9K33 Osa) surface-to-air missile systems destined for Hezbollah is believed to have been targeted. No casualties are reported.

- **July 5, 2013** – Latakia Port: A warehouse containing 50 Russian-made P-800 Yakhont anti-ship missiles is targeted, fearing the missiles could be transferred to Hezbollah. Several Syrian troops are killed and wounded.

- **May 5, 2013** – Al-Hamah: The 104th and 105th Brigades of the Syrian Republican Guard as well as an ammunition warehouse belonging to the 14th Special Forces Division are targeted. Several dead and injured are reported.

- **May 5, 2013** – Mt. Qasioun: Syrian Republican Guard artillery emplacements are struck. Several dead and injured are reported.

- **May 5, 2013** – Al-Dimas, Qadsiya, Al-Saboura, and Jamraya: SA-17 (Buk-M2E) medium-range surface-to-air missile system or unspecified surface-to-surface missiles are believed to be targeted en route to Hezbollah. Several are reported dead and injured.

- **May 2/3, 2013** – Damascus International Airport: A warehouse containing Iranian-made Fateh-110 and Scud D surface-to-surface missiles destined for Hezbollah is believed to have been targeted. No casualties are reported.

- **January 30, 2013** – Jamraya: A convoy carrying arms to Hezbollah, including a SA-17 (Buk-M2E) medium-range surface-to-air missile battery, is believed to have been targeted. Senior IRGC commander Hussam Hush Nawis (aka Hassan Shateri) is killed.

Ms. ROS-LEHTINEN. Thank you so much, sir.

Dr. Byman.

STATEMENT OF DANIEL L. BYMAN, PH.D., PROFESSOR, SECURITY STUDIES PROGRAM, EDMUND A. WALSH SCHOOL OF FOREIGN SERVICE, GEORGETOWN UNIVERSITY

Mr. BYMAN. Madam Chairman, Ranking Member Deutch, members of the committee, thank you very much for having me here today.

Hezbollah is in a time of transition and this is in large part because of the Syrian civil war. Hezbollah forces have been involved in several of the most important battles in the war and they have proven a vital ally to the Syrian regime due to their skill and their discipline, which are often much greater than those of the Syrian army forces.

Hezbollah has had to expand the overall size of its military wing, and although it was cautious about entering the fray, many Lebanese Shi'a now see it as a defender of their community.

They look at the atrocities that the Islamic State is perpetrating against their co-religionists and believe that a strong Hezbollah is necessary to protect their community.

We see extreme voices within the Lebanese Sunni community including jihadists tied to the Islamic State or al-Nusra, al-Qaeda's affiliate. They see Hezbollah as the leading or top foe they face and they've conducted terrorist attacks on Hezbollah targets in Lebanon and Iranian targets there as well.

Perhaps the biggest negative consequence for Hezbollah though has been the collapse of its regional reputation and the associated prestige it's had in the Arab world.

Almost 10 years ago in 2006, Hassan Nasrallah was one of the most popular men in the Arab world for Hezbollah's military efforts against Israel.

Today, he's widely hated. Hezbollah's involvement in the Syrian civil war has largely made it more cautious about taking on Israel. It's taken close to 1,000 causalities and that's a huge number for a relative small group, and this is putting a strain on the organization.

In addition, the organization's Lebanese constituents have little appetite for yet another confrontation, yet another draining conflict.

This could change, though, for several reasons. One is that if there are setbacks in Lebanon or elsewhere the group would have an incentive to restore its past reputation, and fighting Israel might be one way to do so.

Also, Israel regularly attacks Hezbollah targets in Syria and Lebanon to stop the transfer of advanced weapons, as Tony mentioned, and these strikes have at times killed senior Hezbollah officials and even a senior Iranian official.

This has the potential to escalate though, fortunately, we haven't seen that happen yet. And finally, Hezbollah is loyal to Iran and if there were a collapse in the U.S.-Iran nuclear deal or another source of tension, Hezbollah would be seen as part of the Iranian response.

In my judgement, the close relationship between Hezbollah and Iran is not likely to change with the U.S.-Iran nuclear deal. It is possible that Iran might step up support to Hezbollah, taking advantage of the sanctions relief. But at the same time we must recognize that Iran is diplomatically over stretched.

It's deploying considerable forces in Syria to prop up the Assad regime. It maintains a large and clandestine force in Iraq and it's even established limited ties to the Houthis in Yemen. These are considerable financial commitments.

You couple that at home with the collapse in oil prices and add to that decades of economic mismanagement and this has all come at the same time when ordinary Iranians are expecting an increase in economic prosperity due to the deal.

So those sanctions relief will put more money into Iran's coffers. Iran has many, many demands on these scarce funds and in my judgement the level of support for Hezbollah is not likely to change significantly barring a significant change in the regional situation.

For the United States we face a dilemma. Washington, of course, doesn't want Hezbollah's influence to grow. But at the same time, Hezbollah is one of the most formidable foes of the Islamic State and it is fighting the group effectively in Syria.

A standard recommendation is to build up the Lebanese Armed Forces and to otherwise strengthen the Lebanese state to help it counter Hezbollah and I've argued that for quite some time.

For the most part, though, I think we need to recognize that U.S. efforts to do this have failed. In part, this is linked to some general problems with U.S. training programs. But the bigger problem is that Lebanese leaders don't want to exacerbate tension with Hezbollah right now and as a result they're hesitant to go for any efforts to try to push them in that direction.

Part of this is due to fear but Lebanon's situation right now is quite precarious and the country is, I would say, on edge because of the neighboring unrest in Syria.

The million plus Syrian refugees in Lebanon are a potential destabilizing force and I think U.S. aid for the refugees in Lebanon is vital.

We really don't need another failed state in the Middle East and Lebanon, unfortunately, is a fairly strong candidate to be the next one should things get worse.

And finally, as the United States steps up its intervention in Syria and Iraq, continues its efforts to fight Hezbollah, coordination with Israel is going to be essential.

The two countries work well together on this and we need to redouble cooperation to make the most of everything.

Thank you very much.

[The prepared statement of Mr. Byman follows:]

Hezbollah's Growing Threat Against U.S. National Security Interests in the Middle East

Prepared Testimony of Daniel Byman

Professor and Senior Associate Dean, Edmund A. Walsh School of Foreign Service at Georgetown University

Director of Research, Center for Middle East Policy at the Brookings Institution

House Committee on Foreign Affairs
Subcommittee on the Middle East and North Africa

March 22, 2016

Chairman Ros-Lehtinen, Ranking Member Deutch, members of this distinguished subcommittee, and subcommittee staff, thank you for the opportunity to testify today.

Founded over thirty years ago, the Lebanese Hizballah is one of the most powerful and dangerous rebel and terrorist groups in the world. Hizballah, however, is in a time of transition. The Syrian civil war in particular has transformed the group, undermining its position in Lebanon, altering its focus in the region, and tarnishing its image in the Middle East. The group remains a threat to the United States and particularly to Israel, but the tentative deterrence Israel has established is likely to hold, though many factors could upset this uneasy peace. For now, Hizballah has even less interest in a direct clash with the United States. However, the group's close relationship with Iran and ideological opposition to a U.S. role in the Middle East are both factors that could lead to problems in the future. In addition, Hizballah supports an array of local actors in Iraq, Syria, and the Palestinian territories that are or could be opposed to U.S. interests in the Middle East.

My testimony today will detail how and why Hizballah has transformed in recent years with particular attention to the Syrian civil war. It then describes Iranian support for the group in general and in the aftermath of the U.S.-Iran nuclear agreement. My statement then examines Hizballah's declining regional image and assesses the threat to Israel and the United States. My statement concludes by offering several implications for U.S. policy.

Hizballah in Transition

Since the group was founded in the early 1980s, the Lebanese Hizballah has survived, and often triumphed over, numerous challenges to its authority and very existence. Israel has assassinated several of Hizballah's leaders and fought wars of varying intensity against the group since its founding. Hizballah has also faced down numerous challenges in Lebanon, emerging as the strongest political and military organization in the country – including the Lebanese Armed Forces. The Lebanese army currently is not strong enough to crack down on the group, and should it do so, it would further split this already-divided country.

Hizballah has moved away from a number of its historic objectives. Some of this change is due to a maturing of the group and a diminishment of its ideological fervor, but the group's victories have also altered it. With its devastating 1983 bombings of the U.S. embassy in Beirut and the Marine barracks, it succeeded in expelling U.S. troops from Lebanon. Hizballah forces fought Israeli troops in Lebanon and, in 2000, expelled them from the country. Hizballah's original fervor to create an Iranian-style theocracy in Lebanon has dimmed, and it has accepted the reality that it will not bring an Islamic revolution to Lebanon. However, the organization remains bitterly anti-Israel and anti-American.

Hizballah is a terrorist group, but terrorism is only a small part of what the organization does. It is a political party, a social welfare agency, a quasi-state military, and even a part of the Lebanese government. Conceptualizing it only as a terrorist group misses most of its functions and obscures the reason it is so popular among many Lebanese Shi'ites. Unlike many terrorist groups, Hizballah cares about the welfare of its constituents and has deep ties to the Lebanese Shi'ite community. Its hospitals, schools, and social welfare organizations serve Lebanese Shi'ites and at times other communities. However, Hizballah's various functions are interrelated: Hizballah's social welfare organizations feed recruits to its military, and it uses its political power in Lebanon to shield itself from international pressure to disarm. Indeed, Hizballah and its allies' political position gives it veto power over government policy: a power they have used to remove a Prime Minister whom they did not believe was protecting the group's interests. The group's political and military leadership is unified and should be considered part of one cohesive organization: European attempts to ban Hizballah's "military" wing but not its "political" wing misconstrue the nature of the group.

The organization's post-2011 involvement in the Syria civil war has been transformative. Historically the organization presented itself as an Islamist (not Shi'ite) movement dedicated to fighting the West in general and Israel in particular. This image always fell short of reality, but many Lebanese and Arabs in general admired the group for its anti-Israel efforts and services to non-Shi'ites in Lebanon. It seemed to live up to its rhetoric of transcending sectarianism.

Hizballah joined the fray in Syria because the Assad regime has long been a key supporter for its operations in Lebanon and against Israel, as well as a useful transit route for weapons. Even more important, Hizballah's closest ally, Iran was calling in all its favors and saw the potential fall of its ally in Damascus as a calamity. By taking sides in a brutal sectarian war, Hizballah has deepened its Shi'ite identity at the cost of its broader Islamist one and become the sectarian actor it always claimed to transcend.

The organization's position in Lebanon has changed as well. Even before the Syrian civil war, Hizballah angered many Lebanese when it stayed close to Syria after the United States, France, and other powers coerced Syrian forces into leaving Lebanon in 2005. Its firm support for Syria angered many Lebanese Christians and Sunni Muslims opposed to Damascus and in favor of a more independent Lebanon: the pro- and anti-Syrian position became the largest political fault line in Lebanon. Relations with other groups in Lebanon worsened further when, in 2008, Hizballah seized parts of West Beirut after the government tried to wrest control of the group's telecommunication infrastructure. The revelations from the United Nations investigation that Hizballah was probably behind the 2005 assassination of the anti-Syrian Prime Minister Rafik Hariri further worsened relations.[1]

The Syrian civil war that broke out in 2011 took this tension to a new level.[2] Hizballah initially hid its involvement in the war, fearing the further rupturing of ties to anti-Syrian factions in Lebanon. However, the casualty toll became impossible to hide, and in May 2013 its leaders openly embraced its role. Hizballah forces have been involved in several important battles against opposition forces, and they have proven a vital ally for the Syrian regime: their skill and discipline are often far greater than those of Syrian military forces. Hizballah regularly maintains a presence of perhaps 5,000 fighters in Syria, rotating units in and out to maintain overall readiness. Because of the large number of forces it has deployed in Syria, Hizballah has expanded the overall size of its military wing: one analysis puts their number at roughly 20,000 trained fighters, with 5,000 having had advanced training in Iran.[3]

Although Hizballah was cautious about entering the fray, many Lebanese Shi'ites now see it as a defender of their community. They look at the atrocities the Islamic State perpetrates against Shi'ites and other minorities in Syria and Iraq and believe that a strong Hizballah is necessary to protect their community. Occasional anti-Shi'ite violence in Lebanon, rather than intimidate Hizballah, increases support for the group among its core supporters. On the other hand, many Lebanese Sunnis, seeing the Assad regime slaughter their co-religionists on a mass scale next door, now reject a group they once admired for its anti-Israel stance, provision of social services, and relative (by Lebanese standards) lack of corruption. Lebanese Christians and some members of the Sunni middle class are somewhere in the middle, abhorring the Islamic State but still skeptical of Hizballah.

Extreme voices within the Lebanese Sunni community, including jihadists tied to the Islamic State or to Jabhat al-Nusra, Al Qaeda's affiliate in Syria, see Hizballah as a leading or even top foe and have conducted terrorist attacks in Lebanon against the group and its supporters. In 2014, groups probably linked to Jabhat al-Nusra have carried out attacks on Iranian facilities in Lebanon, and in November 2015, Islamic State supporters

---

[1] Ronen Bergman, "The Hezbollah Connection," *New York Times Magazine,* February 10, 2015, http://www.nytimes.com/2015/02/15/magazine/the-hezbollah-connection.html

[2] This section draws on my work with Bilal Saab. See Daniel Byman and Bilal Saab, "Hizballah in a Time

[2] This section draws on my work with Bilal Saab. See Daniel Byman and Bilal Saab, "Hizballah in a Time of Transition," Center for Middle East Policy and Brookings (November 2014,) http://www.brookings.edu/research/papers/2014/11/hezbollah-in-time-of-transition-byman-saab

[3] "Hizbullah," *Jane's World Insurgency and Terrorism,* IIIS.com, May 8, 2015, p. 15.

carried out two suicide bombings in a Hizballah neighborhood in Beirut, killing over 40 people – the worst single bombing Lebanon has suffered since the end of the Lebanese civil war in 1991. Three Lebanese-Americans died in the attack.[4]

Continued Iranian Support

Iranian support has long been vital to Hizballah's survival and success.[5] Indeed, Hizballah entered Syria despite the risks to its reputation and personnel in part to assist its Iranian patron. Hizballah looks to Iran's Supreme Leader, Ayatollah Ali Khamenei, for ideological and strategic direction, and other Iranian officials, including those from the Islamic Revolutionary Guard Corps, regularly offer guidance to the group. Beyond strategic direction, Iran has provided Hizballah with virtually every form of assistance, ranging from arms – including Hizballah's massive rocket and missile arsenal – and money to training and organizational advice. Due to Iranian financing and direct transfers from Iran and Syria, Hizballah's arsenal includes unmanned aerial vehicles, Scud missiles, anti-ship cruise missiles, man-portable air defense systems, anti-tank guided missiles, and other advanced equipment.[6] Financial support is usually said to range between $60 million and $200 million a year, though what counts as support is often not defined and this figure varies depending on the contingencies Hizballah faces. Hizballah has used this money to pay its troops and develop a high-quality social service network. Thousands of Hizballah fighters have also trained in Iran itself. In addition, the foreign networks of Hizballah and those of Iranian intelligence are interwoven, with joint operations being common.[7]

Hizballah leaders have long portrayed themselves as foot soldiers in an Iranian army. Although the group has its own interests that are not linked to Iran's foreign policy – and Iran often respects these differences – the commitment to Tehran's interests is deep and genuine. Tehran, for its part, has a strong and deep commitment to Hizballah and its success in Lebanon. Iran sees the Lebanese group as one of its rare victories in spreading its revolution. In addition, the group offers Iran a way to strike Israel directly. Hizballah also serves as Iran's proxy and ally in the region in general, augmenting its power in Syria and of course Lebanon. The tight coordination of Hizballah and Iranian forces in the Syria fighting has made the already close relationship even closer.

This close relationship is not likely to change with the Joint Comprehensive Plan of Action between the United States and Tehran over the Iranian nuclear program. It is possible that Iran may even step up support for Hizballah, taking advantage of its improved economic position after sanctions relief. With the decline in Iran's relationship with Hamas and the collapse of the Syrian state, Hizballah is one of the few bright spots for Iran in the Arab world, and Tehran wants to keep the group strong. At the same time, Iran is diplomatically overstretched, deploying considerable forces within Syria to prop

---

[4] "3 Dearborn Victims of Lebanon Terror Attack Mourned," November 14, 2015, http://www.detroitnews.com/story/news/local/wayne-county/2015/11/13/dearborn-killed-lebanon-attacks/75716698/

[5] For my thoughts on this issue, see Daniel Byman, *Deadly Connections: States that Sponsor Terrorism* (Cambridge University Press, 2015).

[6] See "Hizbullah," *Jane's World Insurgency and Terrorism.*

[7] For an excellent discussion, see Matthew Levitt, *Hezbollah: The Global Footprint of Iran's Party of God* (Washington, DC: Georgetown University Press, 2015).

up Assad, maintaining a large clandestine presence in Iraq, and even establishing limited ties to the Houthis in Yemen. At home, the collapse of oil prices – and decades of economic mismanagement– has coupled with an increase in popular expectations of economic prosperity among ordinary Iranians. So although sanctions relief puts more money into Iran's coffers, Iran has many demands on these scarce funds, and in my judgment the level of support for Hizballah is not likely to change significantly barring a significant change in the regional situation.

Changing Regional Perceptions of Hizballah

Perhaps the biggest negative consequence for Hizballah in the Syrian civil war is the collapse of its regional reputation and associated prestige in the Arab and broader Muslim world. Hizballah is the only Arab military to defeat Israel by force of arms, which it did when its war of attrition pushed Israel out of Lebanon in 2000. After its 2006 war with Israel, when Hizballah launched perhaps 4,000 rockets and missiles at Israel and fought the Israeli Defense Forces to a draw, opinion polls showed Hizballah's leader, Hassan Nasrallah, as the most popular man in the Arab world. The sectarian nature of the Syrian civil war, however, puts Hizballah firmly on the side of an unpopular minority in the Arab world. Today Nasrallah and Hizballah are regularly vilified, with conservative Sunnis labeling the group the "party of Satan," a twist on the group's name "the party of God."

The March 2016 designation of Hizballah as a terrorist group by the Arab League and Gulf Cooperation Council is a reflection of this shift in attitude. Ironically, Hizballah's use of terrorism as a tactic was much more pronounced in the 1980s, when its suicide bombing of U.S. and French peacekeepers and hostage taking of Westerners in Lebanon was at its peak. Hizballah at the time also worked with Iran to strike targets in the Gulf states because of those regimes' support for Iraq in the Iran-Iraq war. Since then, the organization has consistently been involved in terrorism, often in conjunction with Iran. The League's designation is thus not a reflection of a sudden change in the organization's methods – if anything, the group uses less terrorism if we define the term narrowly to exclude attacks outside war zones and only against civilian targets – but rather a belated attempt by U.S. allies in the Gulf and elsewhere to delegitimize the group and its Iranian backer.

The Threat to Israel

Hizballah remains committed to Israel's destruction, but this goal is less of a priority than in past years. From its inception, Hizballah defined itself as the tip of the spear against Israel, and its forces became progressively more skilled and able to conduct an array of sophisticated military operations against the Jewish state. Its casualty ratio against Israel steadily improved, and Israeli military officers regularly describe the group as formidable. In the 2006 war with Israel, Hizballah killed more than 160 Israelis, a huge figure for the small and casualty-sensitive Jewish state. Hizballah training camps use models of Israeli streets, and the organization's rocket arsenal and tunnel complexes in Lebanon are designed with Israel specifically in mind. All of Israel is in range of

Hizballah's long-range rockets, though Israel's missile defense system offers Israelis some comfort should conflict resume.

Hizballah, often in cooperation with Iran, has conducted an array of terrorist attacks against Israel around the world, including attacks in 1992 and 1994 in Argentina that together killed over 100 people. Hizballah also tried to assassinate Israelis traveling outside their country in Europe and Asia. In 2012, Hizballah was linked to a bus bombing in Bulgaria that killed five Israeli tourists and their Bulgarian driver. Hizballah and Iran often see these attacks as revenge for what they consider to be Israeli aggression, such as the killing of Hizballah leaders or attacks on Iranian nuclear scientists.

In addition to these direct attacks, Hizballah has acted as a quasi-state sponsor of terrorism. Hizballah remains vehement in its calls for Israel's destruction and support for the Palestinian cause. It has supported an array of Palestinian militant groups with training and arms, encouraging them to use violence against Israel. However, several Palestinian groups, notably Hamas, oppose Hizballah's position in Syria and have distanced themselves from the group and its Iranian patron. Shared interests, and the relatively few allies that Hamas and Hizballah possess, however, are likely to ensure that relations are maintained and perhaps even improved should the sectarian fervor in the region die down.

Since 2006 – and in reality well before that – Hizballah has been deterred from a massive attack on Israel. Hizballah fears a fierce Israeli response that would destroy its military infrastructure and devastate the lives and livelihoods of its Lebanese constituents. Because of this fear, Hizballah has looked for ways to continue the conflict with Israel on the margins, keeping the struggle alive but trying to limit the violence to prevent tough Israeli retaliation. Israel, for its part, has been content with a shadow war, where at times it kills a Hizballah commander or destroys a weapons shipment but avoids more aggressive, potentially escalatory actions.[8]

Since 2006, the border has been surprisingly quiet, suggesting the strength of Israel's current deterrence. In addition, the presence of UN peacekeepers deployed after the 2006 war makes it difficult for Hizballah to have the large-scale presence it had in the border area before the war, though it still has cadre there who are not in uniform. Hizballah has built bunkers, underground rocket platforms, and other sites farther away from the border, near the Litani River. Israel has also shot Hizballah fighters in Syria when they attempted to plant a bomb near a border fence along the Golan Heights.[9]

Hizballah's involvement in the Syrian civil war has made it even more cautious about taking on Israel. Hizballah's large-scale deployments in Syria, and the associated casualties – close to 1,000 – are draining the organization.[10] Hizballah has had to expand recruitment and accept younger fighters. Israeli security officials are rightly concerned that Hizballah fighters have gained valuable combat experience. However, they are primarily doing counterinsurgency operations and would face difficultly adjusting to the

---

[8] See Daniel Byman, *A High Price: The Triumphs and Failures of Israeli Counterterrorism* (New York: Oxford University Press, 2012).

[9] "Hizbullah," *Jane's World Insurgency and Terrorism,* pp. 7 and 41.

[10] Ali Alfoneh, "Hezbollah Fatalities in the Syrian War," Washington Institute for Near East Policy, February 22, 2016, http://www.washingtoninstitute.org/policy-analysis/view/hezbollah-fatalities-in-the-syrian-war

high-intensity and overwhelming firepower the Israeli military would bring to any battle. Perhaps most importantly, the organization's Lebanese constituents have little appetite for more conflict.

This caution could change for several reasons. Setbacks in Lebanon or elsewhere would give the group an incentive to restore its past reputation, and fighting Israel is one potentially popular way of doing so. Israel also regularly attacks Hizballah targets in Syria and Lebanon, primarily to stop the transfer of advanced weapons from the Syrian arsenal. These strikes have at times killed senior Hizballah leaders and even a senior Iranian official. Hizballah has not escalated after such attacks, but this restraint is by no means guaranteed. Finally, should the U.S.-Iran nuclear deal collapse and the United States attack the Iranian nuclear infrastructure, Hizballah might attack Israel as part of the Iranian response. Similarly, if U.S.-Iran tension increases for other reasons, we should expect Hizballah to stand by its Iranian ally, and one way of doing so might be to try to drag Israel into a conflict and thus attempt to delegitimize any U.S. response.

Hizballah's has been cautious about a direct confrontation with the United States since the U.S. withdrawal from Lebanon, but it has remained hostile and supportive of anti-U.S. forces in the Middle East. It has assisted Iranian anti-U.S. operations, notably the 1996 Khobar Towers attack that killed 19 U.S. servicemen.[11] When U.S. forces were fighting against Shi'ite militias in Iraq after the 2003 invasion, Hizballah often aided these militias with training and other forms of support. It has also worked with Iran to case U.S. targets around the world and otherwise maintains considerable potential to conduct terrorist attacks should its calculations change. This might occur should there be a U.S.-Iran military confrontation or if the United States decides to try to remove the Assad regime.

Implications for the United States

In Lebanon and Syria, the United States faces a dilemma. Washington correctly does not want Hizballah's regional or national influence to grow. However, Hizballah is one of the most formidable foes of the Islamic State at a time when the United States is both trying to fight the group in Syria and stop the violence from spreading to Lebanon. Hizballah is also reportedly assisting various Shi'ite forces in Iraq against the Islamic State.

A standard recommendation – one I have endorsed in the past and still favor to some degree – is to build up the Lebanese Armed Forces and otherwise strengthen the Lebanese state. Helping the Lebanese state become militarily stronger and better able to provide services would undermine some support for Hizballah and enable the government to resist Hizballah's threats of force that ensure the group's independence. For the most part U.S. efforts to do so have failed, in part due to general problems with U.S. training programs but especially because Lebanese leaders do not want to exacerbate tensions within Lebanon through open hostility toward Hizballah. Part of this is due to

---

[11] Adam Goldman, "Hezbollah Operative Indicted in United States for Attack on Khobar Towers," *Washington Post*, August 26, 2015, https://www.washingtonpost.com/world/national-security/hezbollah-operative-indicted-in-us-for-attack-on-khobar-towers-captured/2015/08/26/6f84ad08-4c00-11c5-902f-39e9219e574b_story.html

fear, but part is also a concern that Lebanon's precarious stability could collapse should Lebanese elites further divide the country as waves of unrest emanate from Syria.

The Saudi decision to pull $4 billion in support from Lebanon (most of which was to go to its armed forces), freeze funding of suspected Hizballah bank accounts in the Kingdom, and discourage Saudis from using Lebanon as a tourist destination further consolidates Hizballah's position. Riyadh, facing significant budget shortfalls due to the decline in the price of oil, is waging an expensive effort of its own in Yemen. Saudi Arabia's deficit in 2015 was almost $100 billion, and the Yemeni war is costing it at least $1 billion per month (the true figure is probably much more).[12] Hizballah has roundly criticized the Saudi war in Yemen as well as Riyadh's execution of the dissident Shi'ite cleric Nimr al-Nimr. The refusal of the Lebanese government to openly side with Saudi Arabia against Iran in Syria and Yemen or to condemn the January 2016 attack on the Saudi embassy in Tehran – in large part because Lebanese leaders did not want to anger Hizballah – has led Riyadh to question whether its money was buying friendship. Saudi support had enabled anti-Hizballah figures to maintain some degree of power and patronage with the military and Lebanese society in general, and its diminishment offers Hizballah a relative advantage. The United States should encourage Riyadh to resume its support for non-Hizballah individuals and institutions in Lebanon.

The million plus Syrian refugees in Lebanon are a potential destabilizing force that could lead to more violence in the fragile country. The refugees might take part in the fighting in Syria, with Lebanon serving as a base and a haven. It is also possible that the refugees might incite violence in Lebanon, fostering a civil war, as the Palestinians did before them. To prevent this, more U.S. and international aid for refugees in Lebanon is vital. The United States should also assist Lebanon in securing its borders and otherwise trying to prevent the Syrian conflict from spilling over into the country.

Finally, the United States should work with Israel to ensure its deterrence of Hizballah and that its limited uses of force in Syria and elsewhere do not escalate into a broader confrontation. Should the U.S. step up its role in Syria and Iraq, and thus interact indirectly with Hizballah-linked forces, tight coordination with Israel becomes especially important.

[12] Mohamad Bazzi, "Why the Oil Collapse Is Forcing Saudi Arabia to Cut Back on Its Checkbook Diplomacy," *Reuters,* March 16, 2016, http://blogs.reuters.com/great-debate/2016/03/16/why-oil-collapse-is-forcing-saudi-arabia-to-cut-back-on-its-checkbook-diplomacy/

Ms. ROS-LEHTINEN. Thank you very much to all of you. I'll start the questions. When the Lebanese justice minister resigned he stated that Hezbollah's undue influence was ruining Lebanon's relations with Arab nations.

Saudi cut its military aid to Lebanon. Hezbollah still wields considerable clout in the Lebanese Government. How can the U.S. ensure that Iran and Hezbollah do not gain even more influence in Lebanon and given Hezbollah's relationship with the Lebanese Armed Forces should the United States reassess the President's budget request for $105 million in foreign military financing for Lebanon? Dr. Levitt.

Mr. LEVITT. I think one of the significant steps that U.S. agencies have taken recently is an effort to take the financial fight to Beirut where Hezbollah until recently has been banking with impunity.

The Treasury Department has been targeting designations that go right back to the heart of Beirut and we know that that's having an impact because Hassan Nasrallah is telling us so.

So in several of his last speeches including in particular in December in that speech he used I think 23 out of 55 minutes to deny that Hezbollah has any businesses whatsoever which, of course, it does. They're just not listed as Hezbollah, Incorporated.

Now, armed with the Hezbollah International Financing Prevention Act, U.S. agencies are really truly empowered to, in the administration's words, thwart the group's network at every turn by imposing sanctions on financial institutions that deal with Hezbollah or key elements.

Tony hit the nail on the head. The ability of Hezbollah to use Beirut as the core, as the hub of its literally international organized criminal activities threatens Lebanon's financial system, which is the backbone of its economy.

We can help Lebanon protect that financial system, not undermine it—to the contrary protect it, and when you speak to Lebanese officials who are outside of Hezbollah they beg for that assistance.

Mr. BADRAN. I would just add just a couple of points. First, more broadly, we have to understand—I mean, it's hard to say this but we have to understand that there is a big level of complicity, unfortunately, with Hezbollah's criminal acts.

So corruption is widespread and it has affected every corner of the Lebanese economy down to the micro level. Think of Florida with the cartels, right, and the drug money that went through. It corrupts and it infiltrates segments—banks and other parts of the economy.

It's a similar situation, unfortunately, and they have key positions and they're very keen on guarding these key positions that enable them to do this in the government. I mentioned the customs office, financial auditor, general security, et cetera, et cetera.

So dealing with Lebanon as though there's a separation between Lebanon and Hezbollah becomes increasingly difficult. So we cannot have kid gloves sort of when we're dealing with this situation.

The Lebanese have to be placed—you know, facing a tough choice or else this is going to continue indefinitely. With the LAF, similar things. Why—the Saudi recognition that ultimately the LAF is acting as an auxiliary as opposed to sort of a challenge to Hezbollah has made them reach the conclusion we cannot continue to fund this uncritically. There has to be an assessment as to how to separate operationally Hezbollah from the LAF and also to put the LAF in front of its own responsibilities in safeguarding the United Nations' Security Council Resolution 1701 or simply in the way it's rounding up Sunni young men and just putting them in jail and exacerbating tensions in the country when they're supposed to be a national institution.

So just a couple of thoughts. I think that an assessment is certainly due in this case.

Ms. Ros-Lehtinen. Thank you.

Mr. Byman. One concern I have is that by the Saudi withdrawal of aid if the U.S. were to reduce support for the Lebanese Armed Forces that the winner would be Hezbollah—that these institutions and Saudi funding that goes to various places in Lebanon have tremendous flaws—overwhelming flaws. But they're better than the alternative, which is an unfettered Hezbollah.

And so I would agree strongly that assessing this regularly is necessary but we should encourage the Saudis to resume their aid.

We want countervailing forces to Hezbollah in Lebanon and I think U.S. ties to Lebanese Armed Forces are also necessary even though we need to recognize that the Lebanese army is going to be limited and that's a very polite way of saying that they're not going to be able to accomplish what we want.

Ms. Ros-Lehtinen. Thank you. And my last question is Russia's role. Hezbollah may have advanced Russian weapon systems. Iran is believed to have transferred some of these to Hezbollah.

Russia is also working with Iran and Hezbollah to support the Assad regime in Syria and protect its own interests. What can you tell us about the Russian-Hezbollah relationship and what that might mean for the U.S. and for Israel?

Mr. Levitt. If you want to be polite there's just a de facto relationship between Russia and Hezbollah in their cooperative support together with Iran for the Assad regime.

I'd argue it's much more than that. You effectively have Russian air cover for the entire pro-Assad axis which very much includes Hezbollah, as Dan mentioned.

But it goes much farther than that. It's not just the obvious things we can see when we're paying attention to the news and to what Russia is doing in the region, and while they may have removed some assets from the region they haven't removed as many as they said they had and Putin himself has been quite blunt to the fact that they can put them back very quickly.

I'm no less concerned about some of the illicit procurement efforts that I alluded to earlier in Europe in particular that are happening including in places like the former Soviet Union.

Consider the case of Ali Fayyad who, at our request, was arrested by the Czechs, a dual Lebanese-Ukrainian citizen who was procuring all kinds of former Soviet Union arms for Hezbollah.

Hezbollah took notice because Ali Fayyad is important to them and they kidnapped five people in Lebanon and eventually those people were released. Ali Fayyad was released.

We still have fingers into this investigation because Ali Fayyad was arrested together with two Ivorians, dual Lebanese Ivorian citizens who are still in custody in the Czech Republic, and while it remains to be seen if anything will really happen with it, last week the Lebanese Government announced that they are actually intending to prosecute Ali Fayyad, who was sent from the Czech Republic back to Lebanon on arms procurement weapons trafficking charges, not mentioning the T word, terrorism, the H word, Hezbollah, of course.

But this would be a step forward in demonstrating there might be some elements of the Lebanese Government with which we can partner with more than others.

Mr. BADRAN. I mentioned earlier the Israeli concern regarding Hezbollah operational experience by working side to side with the Russians in Syrian.

Because they have gained experience in combined arms operations and working with new weapons systems that the Russians introduced to the Syrian theater Russian trainers that are working with the Syrian military and Hezbollah sitting there and watching they have also with the Iranians started a joint operations room in Iraq last year to exchange intelligence.

So we hear about the Russian communication with the Israelis on one hand to deconflict in Syria but there's also a parallel sort of relationship that the Russians are maintaining with the Iranians who are really the ground troops of the Russian air force in Syria.

So the Russians, you know, when they're providing close air support in Aleppo it's—none of the IRGC and Hezbollah were on the ground checking around.

Now, if this situation transfers—the fear was that this situation would transfer to the south of Syria in the Golan. Now, thankfully, it hasn't happened yet. Maybe it will not happen. Maybe the Russians will balance out their relationship with the Israelis and that with the Iranians.

But nevertheless it's a risk that should the Russians say we are going to combat terrorist groups in southern Syria near Jordan, near Israel, who are going to be the ground troops for such an operation? It's going to be the IRGC and Hezbollah.

So, clearly, the coast is not yet clear for Israel. For now, the Russian announcement that they're going to kind of freeze their operations for a while or reorient them elsewhere it doesn't seem to include the south of Syria yet. But it's by no means, I don't think, sort of gone—should be stricken out of our calculation that something like that is going to happen in the future.

Mr. BYMAN. I'll only briefly add that I'm very skeptical about the degree to which Russia is going to cease its operations. I think there will be still considerable support and the number of assets that have been redeployed so far have been quite limited.

I will also add, however, that Russia has a visceral distrust and dislike of anything that smacks of Islamic extremism and the Russians are if anything pragmatic but at the same time they see that broader community as quite hostile and they are quite concerned.

Ms. ROS-LEHTINEN. Thank you very much.

Mr. Deutch of Florida.

Mr. DEUTCH. Thank you, Madame Chairman.

Dr. Byman, you had said—you described Nasrallah's current position as one who's widely hated. You also pointed out that Hezbollah is a formidable foe of Islamic State.

Do those two things—is it likely that because they are a formidable foe of ISIS that that will have some impact on the way Nasrallah is viewed?

How do those interrelate and on the ground, more broadly, how does the population view Hezbollah, given the role they've played in fighting ISIS?

Mr. BYMAN. For most people in the Middle East the primary fight is not between the Islamic State and the United States but rather between the Syrian regime and what we would call the moderate opposition.

It's not a term I love because it means 100 different things. But that said, Hezbollah has been an arm of the Syrian regime, killing its own people including a range of groups supported by the United States which whom we have, I think, reasonable relations and Hezbollah is widely hated in the Sunni Arab world because it is seen as on the side of an oppressive minority regime that has killed several hundred thousand of its own people. It's a staggering number.

Hezbollah's operations against the Islamic State for most people in the region are a footnote to this, right, where some would say that's bad, some would say that's good. But they would focus on their killing of people they regard as much more mainstream and much more heroic figures and much more representative.

So that, to me, is the primary reason for its unpopularity and that's, to me, why so many Arab states that are backing the moderate opposition are against Hezbollah is they see it really as an enemy and a tool of Iran.

Mr. DEUTCH. And does—the decision by GCC and the Arab League to designate Hezbollah a terrorist organization what's the impact of that in the region and do you expect another—are there retaliatory attacks to come from the designation? What happens next?

Mr. BYMAN. I think at this point the designation is really a reflection of the political reality on the ground rather than a major shift.

These states have been tremendously against Hezbollah for a while. The designation helps, though, right. It enables us to garner diplomatic support. A number of things that Matt has mentioned, for example, are helped diplomatically by being able to point to a GCC or an Arab League designation to kind of push along agendas we want.

So I think it's a relatively small impact but nevertheless symbolic of a bigger shift.

Mr. DEUTCH. And does the failure—I'll throw this open to anyone on the panel—does the failure on the part of Europe to designate Hezbollah—I mean, what does it actually mean?

What are they able to do from a fund-raising standpoint? What are they able to do from an operational standpoint that could potentially be stopped if Europe actually does the right thing and designates them a terrorist organization?

Dr. Levitt.

Mr. LEVITT. Yes. Everything. Right now for an EU designation of Hezbollah you have to make a definitive link to the terrorist and military wing.

But Hezbollah's no fool. In fact, they're quite good at layering and obfuscation. So they engage in all kinds of activities. They just don't put a Hezbollah shingle out there.

The only case we've had since the designation was not an EU action but a German action against the Orphan Welfare Foundation, which was a Hamas front organization and was caught making the mistake of openly providing some of its donations to the Martyrs Foundation, which can be tied, though some Europeans would even disagree with this, directly to militancy.

So designation wise, the EU can't really do very much. It does provide an umbrella so that if member states want to do something they can say well, Hezbollah is at least partially designated—if you can find that they're doing arms procurement, arms procurement, for example, is by definition probably not for social welfare or political activity. So you can feel more comfortable doing that.

I would argue they should feel comfortable doing it anyway since it's black and white criminal activity. Quietly on law enforcement issues we've seen great cooperation. But the designation as such doesn't actually empower them to do a whole lot.

Mr. DEUTCH. But what would the full designation empower them to do?

Mr. LEVITT. If they found someone or something that was doing anything for Hezbollah and all you'd have to prove was Hezbollah that entity could be designated.

Mr. DEUTCH. And what would that mean to——

Mr. LEVITT. Asset freezes, travel bans.

Mr. DEUTCH. Right. And in terms of—in terms of impacting their operations, what would the impact be?

Mr. LEVITT. Given the huge increase in Hezbollah operations in Europe including a whole bunch of entities that we have designated, that the DOJ has indicted there's very good reason to think that a designation in the EU would empower European nations to target those activities in Europe.

Let me put it to you another way. Since the July 2013 partial designation of Hezbollah, Hezbollah activities in Europe have increased. I'm writing a study on it right now.

So that suggests that maybe Hezbollah has kind of called that bluff and by activities I don't only mean fund raising, logistics and procurement but operations as well as evidenced from the—not just the first Cyprus operation which was predesignation but the second one with over eight tons of explosive materiel which we believe was going to be sent farther into Europe.

Mr. DEUTCH. And Mr. Badran—last question, Madam Chairman.

Is there any—can you foresee anything that would prompt or what would—that would prompt the Europeans to take the necessary step, given what Dr. Levitt just laid out, to make this a full designation?

Mr. BADRAN. I remain a little—I mean, Matt has expressed more optimism and I hope—and he would know, certainly, better than me on this—I hope it actually goes in this direction.

But one of the things, for instance, let's take what the GCC has done, right, and let's actually help them enforce it and provide also reassurances for these very vulnerable nations that the United States will stand with them as they push against any Iranian and Hezbollah retaliation.

But one of the things, for instance, that they're looking to do and that could be transferred into the European context just as easily because it's not just front organizations that are involved here.

The Saudis leaked, when they made their decision—the Saudis leaked through the Lebanese media that one of the things they might consider is actually going after not just Shi'ite businessmen that may have ties to Hezbollah's financial operations but also Christian businessmen who have interests in the Gulf states and those are a lot and they're big interests, including—they even went so far as to leak that this includes sitting ministers in the Lebanese cabinet, okay—that they're willing to go that far I think they waved it as a threat.

We should encourage them to follow through on all of this because there's a huge amount, especially in the United Arab Emirates, of financial interests for people who are on the face of it legitimate businessmen, both Shi'ite and Christian and Sunni even. In Kuwait especially there are Sunni Kuwaiti businessmen especially with tremendous ties to Hezbollah's financial empire.

This is an opportunity to take to squeeze and then to transfer the same template to the Europeans if they're willing to go along with it.

Mr. DEUTCH. Thank you very much. Thank you, Madam Chair.

Ms. ROS-LEHTINEN. Thank you, Mr. Deutch.

Mr. Boyle of Pennsylvania.

Mr. BOYLE. Thank you. I just have a few questions. When I was in Israel last August—well, actually, a few years ago and then again last August, folks I talked to including Israeli generals talked—they said not if there's a third Lebanon war but when there's a third Lebanon war, and that really struck me.

So my question was about the rockets because there's been quite a change even since I was there 7 months ago. The Israeli military that was briefing us had used the figure about 85,000 rockets. Then it was revised upwards after that to 100,000 and now I read upwards of 150,000.

So I guess two questions. First, where exactly do things stand now in terms of the amount of rockets and their sophistication. As I recall from 2006, the rockets that they had were not exactly precise.

So that's the number one, and then number two is what is our best intelligence that would be the event to trigger a third Lebanon war?

So I decided to ask all my questions at once and then leave it to each of you to figure it out which ones you'll want to take.

Mr. LEVITT. Thanks for those questions.

I don't know any Israeli security or military official who doesn't talk that way, not because they're looking to invite a third Lebanon war but because you don't stockpile—the numbers I hear are 130,000 to 150,000 rockets—to keep them as paperweights.

I don't think that they want to initiate. I had an opportunity to speak to a senior Israeli official this week. He said, we will not initiate but we will not allow Nasrallah to threaten the entire country, as he puts it, not just the north with all of these weapons.

And what we're dealing with now are more sophisticated weapons than we saw in 2006, both an increase in the number of actual guided systems and also maybe even more significantly because not all rockets are equal and the majority of their arsenal is not this longer—medium and longer range guided missiles but the GPS kits that they are reportedly getting from Iran which you can put on something like which they had in the past and you can make a dumb rocket smarter.

They're trying to cope with a situation where hundreds of rockets are fired at specific buildings in Tel Aviv and one can understand why they won't tolerate that type of a situation and as Tony said why they've made it very clear from a deterrent perspective that if it happens their response will be much more severe than it has been in the past.

Mr. BADRAN. So Matt covered the issue of the long range rockets that they've upgraded them—they're now precision guided. They're no longer dumb rockets. Now they can hit strategic installations.

They've added also the Russian-made anti-ship—the cruise missile. Now, those are very, very dangerous. They can hit strategic installations offshore, installation gas rigs, et cetera.

So the Israelis have now taken this in such that it's part of their doctrine, that they're emphasizing defense of the interior, which is a departure from what it used to be in the past. It used to be much more offensive minded.

Now they take into consideration that the population is going to have to suffer and there's going to be prioritization as to what has to be guarded by the Iron Dome missile defense system because of the high density of the weapons—of the rockets that Hezbollah can fire on a daily basis, basically about 1,000 a day.

Now, not all of these are long range—okay, a lot of them are actually the shorter range. But there's 1 million other issues now.

All of this stuff that they're learning in Syria is going to be translated kinetically in the next war in maybe offensive operations into the Galilee because now they're on the Golan Heights, not just in Lebanon.

So you ask what would trigger such a war. See, this is where the failure of U.S. policy in Syria becomes something about much more than just Syria.

The Israelis are now warning that any solution to the Syrian crisis cannot leave Iran in a position of dominance in Syria and in a position on the Golan Heights.

Unfortunately, the United States—the U.S. President has said that any solution in Syria has to take into consideration respecting Iranian equities in Syria. So you can see where now our policy in Syria and Israel's position in Syria are directly at odds.

Any position, any movement in the Golan, any movement of rockets or strategic weapons across the border into Lebanon has the potential for triggering such a conflict and the more they entrench themselves in Syria the shorter this time period becomes of when

Israel—of how long Israel can tolerate this buildup before having to take action.

So the situation in Syria, I think, is critical to the security. Of course, I mean, it affects Turkey, it affects Jordan just the same, but very critical as far as Israeli security is concerned.

Mr. BOYLE. My time has expired so I thank the chair and the ranking member.

Ms. ROS-LEHTINEN. Thank you so much.

And Dr. Levitt, you wanted to say something and you had run out of time. So this is a great opportunity right now. Grab it.

Mr. LEVITT. Thank you so much.

I don't want to take much time because I've actually managed to sneak most of it in.

But I did want to just add just as an example of some of the things that are being done creatively and some of the European co-operation we're getting, under the Counterterrorism Partnership Fund, the State Department together with DOJ and others have been able to put together a series—an international initiative to raise awareness about Iran and Hezbollah's broad range of terrorist and criminal activities around the world, engaging with partners around the world, not only informing them and teaching them but then teaching them how to use tools at their disposal and we're seeing actual cases come out of these including, for example, the U.S. co-led law enforcement coordination group, which we co-lead with EUROPOL, getting EUROPOL to focus on Hezbollah activities.

There are EUROPOL cases now. This is not a small achievement. Clearly, there is much, much more to be done but I see an interest in the part of Europeans because of Hezbollah's increased activities there, because of Hezbollah's regional growth and in particular in Syria and figuring out what they can do within their system, within their designation partial regime to work with us on this target.

Ms. ROS-LEHTINEN. Thank you.

And gentlemen, are there any parting thoughts that you would like to leave us with? Mr. Deutch?

Mr. DEUTCH. No, thank you, ma'am.

Ms. ROS-LEHTINEN. Well, thank you very much. This subcommittee is very concerned about doing everything that we can to cut off the funding to this terrorist organization.

We're going to keep on in that track. Thank you. And with that, the subcommittee is adjourned. Thank you to everyone.

[Whereupon, at 4:44 p.m., the subcommittee was adjourned.]

APPENDIX

MATERIAL SUBMITTED FOR THE RECORD

SUBCOMMITTEE HEARING NOTICE
COMMITTEE ON FOREIGN AFFAIRS
U.S. HOUSE OF REPRESENTATIVES
WASHINGTON, DC 20515-6128

Subcommittee on the Middle East and North Africa
Ileana Ros-Lehtinen (R-FL), Chairman

March 18, 2016

TO: MEMBERS OF THE COMMITTEE ON FOREIGN AFFAIRS

You are respectfully requested to attend an OPEN hearing of the Committee on Foreign Affairs, to be held by the Subcommittee on the Middle East and North Africa in Room 2172 of the Rayburn House Office Building (and available live on the Committee website at http://www.ForeignAffairs.house.gov):

DATE: Tuesday, March 22, 2016

TIME: 2:30 p.m.

SUBJECT: Hezbollah's Growing Threat Against U.S. National Security Interests in the Middle East

WITNESSES: Matthew Levitt, Ph.D.
Director and Fromer-Wexler Fellow
Stein Program on Counterterrorism and Intelligence
Washington Institute for Near East Policy

Mr. Tony Badran
Research Fellow
Foundation for Defense of Democracies

Daniel L. Byman, Ph.D.
Professor
Security Studies Program
Edmund A. Walsh School of Foreign Service
Georgetown University

By Direction of the Chairman

The Committee on Foreign Affairs seeks to make its facilities accessible to persons with disabilities. If you are in need of special accommodations, please call 202/225-5021 at least four business days in advance of the event, whenever practicable. Questions with regard to special accommodations in general (including availability of Committee materials in alternative formats and assistive listening devices) may be directed to the Committee.

COMMITTEE ON FOREIGN AFFAIRS

MINUTES OF SUBCOMMITTEE ON _____ *the Middle East and North Africa* _____ HEARING

Day____*Tuesday*____ Date____*March 22, 2016*____ Room_____*2172*_____

Starting Time ____*3:48 p.m.*____ Ending Time ____*4:43 p.m.*____

Recesses | *0* | (____to____) (____to____) (____to____) (____to____) (____to____) (____to____)

Presiding Member(s)

Chairman Ros-Lehtinen

Check all of the following that apply:

Open Session ☑   Electronically Recorded (taped) ☑
Executive (closed) Session ☐   Stenographic Record ☑
Televised ☑

TITLE OF HEARING:

Hezbollah's Growing Threat Against U.S. National Security Interests in the Middle East

---

SUBCOMMITTEE MEMBERS PRESENT:

Chairman Ros-Lehtinen, Reps. Issa, Weber, Meadows, Zeldin, Deutch, Grayson, Meng, Frankel, and Boyle

---

NON-SUBCOMMITTEE MEMBERS PRESENT: *(Mark with an * if they are not members of full committee.)*

HEARING WITNESSES: Same as meeting notice attached? Yes ☑ **No** ☐
(If "no", please list below and include title, agency, department, or organization.)

STATEMENTS FOR THE RECORD: *(List any statements submitted for the record.)*

TIME SCHEDULED TO RECONVENE _____
or
TIME ADJOURNED ____*4:43 p.m.*____

Subcommittee Staff Director